MW00512751

If You Want to Be a Better Christian,

TRAIN LIKE A CHAMPION

TOM AND MAUREEN RITARI

ISBN 978-1-0980-8641-1 (paperback)
ISBN 978-1-0980-8642-8 (digital)

Copyright © 2021 by Tom and Maureen Ritari

All rights reserved. No part of this publication may be reproduced, distributed, or transmitted in any form or by any means, including photocopying, recording, or other electronic or mechanical methods without the prior written permission of the publisher. For permission requests, solicit the publisher via the address below.

Christian Faith Publishing, Inc.
832 Park Avenue
Meadville, PA 16335
www.christianfaithpublishing.com

Printed in the United States of America

Contents

Preface...5
Acknowledgments 7
Introduction..9

I

1   If You Want to Be a Better Christian, *Then Train
    like a Champion*...15
2   Being a Good Teammate 25
3   How Can I Be a Better Coach?........................28
4   Discipline of God..36
5   Ben Franklin and the Vessel...........................41
6   Snippets 44
7   In Closing 49
8   Thoughts on 1, 2, and 3 John 50
    1 John...50
        Chapter 1 50
        Chapter 2 52
        Chapter 3 58
        Chapter 4 66
        Chapter 5 69
    2 John...72
    3 John...74

II

9   Soldier or Warrior? 77
10 Do You *Know* Jesus or Just Know of Him? 82
11 Patience and Waiting on God's Timing............84
12 Redeemed 94
13 Obedience..100

PREFACE

The writing of this book is a compilation of many topics, thoughts, and the result of a few years of listening to God and what He desires us to put down on to paper. I began writing a few years ago when I was between jobs, and God spoke to my heart. I was never much of a writer, but when I listened to God, the words seemed to flow. It was then I penned *If You Want to Be a Better Christian, Train like a Champion*. When God speaks to you, you listen. *Train like a Champion* was inspired by many years of experience coaching high school sports and knowing what it takes to win. I then applied those observations to becoming a better Christian and winning a place in heaven, as advised by the apostle Paul in the Amplified version (AMP), saying, "Do you not know that in a race all the runners run [their very best to win], but only one receives the prize? Run [your race] in such a way that you may seize the prize and make it yours!"

There always seemed to be roadblocks to getting that work published, but now I know why. God's timing is always perfect. A few years later, my wife was being directed by God to begin her own writing. She began her work on several different personal development topics.

The words that we have written and the different topics included are not in story format. These thoughts are coming from two individuals, not trained pastors, who are in love with the Lord. We have spent much time in His Word and have read numerous Christian authors. We are not biblical scholars, but we are attempting to bring forth His Word from a layman's perspective.

Other than the segment "If You Want to be a Better Christian," our writings present concise thoughts which are easily read, taken in, ingested, and pondered. We decided to combine our works into one book with the title *The Word from 5794,* which has been our home address for thirty-plus years. It is our hope that you find it an easy but thought-provoking book. We have been called to go out and spread His Word. If you have an interest in our visiting and speaking, we can be contacted at:

Ritari5@hotmail.com
Phone: 440-813-4916 or 440-813-2366

ACKNOWLEDGMENTS

- Lord and Savior Jesus Christ for His word and guiding light.
- My spouse, Maureen, for her support and for being the strong Christian woman.
- Pastor Jack Woods and his daughter, Wendy, for editing this work and their long-term friendship.
- Pastor James Friend of the Rock Church Conneaut, Ohio, our home church.
- Coach Jim McDonald, former Edinboro State University basketball coach, for being a strong Christian leader for the young men in his charge. Later on, he initiated the program MGM (Meeting God through Missions).
- Dr. Mark Maire, brother-in-law, for his guidance and direction.
- All the coaches and pastors who we have come in contact with during our lifetime.

INTRODUCTION

By Tom Ritari

The purpose of writing this book is twofold. One is to bring the Word of God to readers. The second is to reach past and present athletes and those who have a slight interest in athletics. I have experienced both the highs and lows of athletic competition and coaching. My hope is to take principles from the athletic world and apply them to one's walk with Christ. My challenge to the reader is to become a better Christian through the use of athletic terms and training techniques.

Athletics has become an extremely important part of society today. Whether as a participant, coach, or fan, many people have at least a passing interest in athletics as an observer or a participant. The Super Bowl is one of the most watched events year in and year out. People and clubs hold huge parties; office pools total in the hundreds of millions of dollars. People watch not only the game but also the creative advertising that interrupts the flow of the game. Some relive their football experiences and wonder how those talented players do what they do.

Parents, grandparents, and friends attend youngsters' games. T-ball, soccer, junior football, and basketball bring in many spectators. When I attend these events—because I enjoy these events—I watch the adults as much as I observe the young athletes. I always find it interesting to see reactions to bad calls by the referees. I watch to see how they respond to both the good and bad ones. Some parents are extremely encouraging to all, while others are attempting to correct their failures as athletes through their son or daughter.

Participation in sports, when led by a strong, caring coach, has proven time and time again to help provide proper direction to misguided youth. We may question the salaries of professional athletes, but our society has created the situation. The emphasis on winning and thus buying the best available talent is a product of our competitive and business society. College athletes at top Division 1 schools are placed on pedestals by their friends, administration, and sports analysts. This pedestal has even been brought into high school athletics with the televising of athletes signing to college scholarships. It's no wonder some of these athletes have difficulties maintaining a humble spirit.

Unexpected results do occur though. At the professional level, these talented wealthy individuals attract *takers*, or we could use the term *entourage*. Mike Tyson is a great example. Tyson was the heavyweight boxing champion, earning hundreds of millions of dollars. Today, he basically has nothing. Big-time college athletes have been reprimanded by the NCAA for questionable activities. Sport does, however, reflect both good and bad very much like our society does.

Through this book, I will attempt to answer many questions. I believe that God has been the force behind my writing. It is His thoughts and words that flow through these pages.

Some questions I will attempt to respond to are the following:

1. How does being a good athlete relate to being a good Christian?
2. How can I improve my walk with God?
3. What qualities should a good athlete/Christian possess?
4. What qualities should a good Christian coach possess?

In answering these questions, I include an in-depth message on that topic. I have become more of a prolific writer than ever before. It is all-encompassing when I listen to the words God wants me to write. Following the basic chapters, responding to these questions, I have included thoughts and messages God has given me. It is my hope that even if nothing new is revealed to you, these words will further emphasize and encourage your walk with God. The use of biblical passages will vary between direct quoting and references for you at the end of each chapter. I also refuse to give Satan any glory. I will not show him any respect.

I

Tom Ritari

1

If You Want to Be a Better Christian, *Then Train like a Champion*

In my many years of coaching, I have influenced thousands of young people, hopefully in a positive, strong, Christian way. Most of the athletes I have coached have wanted to improve, get better, and be part of the starting team. Every athlete and coach should have goals to strive for, to keep their eyes upon:

- In a race, it's the finish line.
- In basketball, it's the basketball goal.
- In football, it is aptly named *the goal line*.
- To do our best in each and every situation.
- *Winning* is not mentioned, as goals should be performance-based.

As a Christian, our goal is:

- In our time on earth, it's to walk the walk of Christ, our Savior, so we will spend eternity singing His praises in heaven.

Ever watch a good hurdler? In the race, his head never bobs up and down as he hurdles. His eyes are focused on the finish line. Good hurdlers do not even seem to hurdle. A good basketball shooter does not take his eyes off the rim; it does not matter what is going on around Him or if there is a hand in His face. Golfers also keep their heads down and stay focused on the ball. Therefore, our focus should be on the goal that is the prize. Our prize is to spend eternity with our God. Fix your eyes upon Jesus, and the world around you will all pass away.

To develop into a champion athlete, you *must* master the fundamentals. Sometimes it seems like taking baby steps, and frustration sets in when the skill required is not coming quickly. Professional athletes work on fundamentals every day. Their rewards are great, and the professional does not want some rookie bumping him/her out to pasture. I know NBA shooters on game day, before the game, will go out and shoot five hundred shots. They are the best shooters in the whole world.

Do you have that kind of dedication? Or do you allow something to get in your way of being great. The Lord wants greatness for us.

How passionate are you about the game you play? Will that passion carry you through the tough times, the frustrating times, the times your friends call you to go party? Passion and commitment seem to be the same as each causes the other. *Passion = Commitment = Passion.*

Other qualities a champion must have are the following:

- Great attitude in practice = I want to get better every day.
- Can you or will you grow from criticism?
- Follow the training rules?
- Have a basic and, later, a deeper knowledge of the game.
- Have confidence in playing the sport.
- Be unselfish.
- Be disciplined.
- Have some natural ability.
- Respect the authority of coaches and officials.
- Have faith and trust in your teammates.
- Establish goals for yourself in the sport.
- Be in your best possible shape.

Comparing these qualities of a champion to becoming a stronger Christian is easy for me to explain. What are the Christian fundamentals? Are you ready to take baby steps before you take the giant steps?

- Prayer
- Fellowship
- Reading His Word (Bible reading)
- Service

Prayer

What is prayer? Prayer is communication with our heavenly Father. When you were just starting your prayer walk, did you start with "Now I lay me down to sleep..."? If you did or still do, it is a beginning. As you progress in your prayer life, you will find the desire to become a better and stronger Christian. You will find yourself praying for more things and more people. We never outgrow our need for prayer. Our heavenly Father wants daily communication with His children. Oftentimes, prayer is found in chaos or crisis in our lives.

David, in *Psalm 65:2 (New Life Version [NLV])*, says, "Oh you who hears prayer, to you all flesh will come."

From the pen of Jacques-Bénigne Lignel Bousset: "Christianity is the religion of prayer." Thus, to be a Christian is to be one who prays. In other words, prayer is the daily business of a Christian.

Prayer teaches the sovereignty and activity of the living God in whose hands nature is like pliable clay. *Romans 8:3* tells us that the law cannot do what God can do. Answered prayer becomes credible. It changes the natural and psychological order. From *Proverbs 21:1 (New King James Version [NKJV])*: "The king's heart is in the hands of the LORD, like rivers of water: he turns it wherever He wishes" If God is omnipotent and He knows our needs and supplies all of them, then why pray?

1. God's relationship is personal: You and me, parent and child, friend and friend, master and servant, creator and creature.

2. Prayer is the channel of human creativity, casualty, and cooperation with the divine ordaining and overruling.
3. Things are brought to pass most often only as man prays, and without prayer some things do not occur.

> Therefore I exhort, first of all, that supplications, prayers, intercessions and giving of thanks be made for all men; for kings, and for all who are in authority; that we may lead a quiet and peaceable life in all Godliness and reverence. For this is good and acceptable in the sight of God our Savior; Who desires all men to be saved, and to come to the knowledge of truth. *(1 Tim. 2:1–4 [New King James Version (NKJV)])*

Prayer is communication, a desire to enter into conscious and intimate relationship with God, who is our life *(Ps. 63:1–8, Ps. 73:25–26, Luke 6:12, 1 John 1:3)*. God hungers for our fellowship *(Rev. 3:20)*. Prayer or thanksgiving is the outpouring of gratitude to God because of His grace, mercy, and loving-kindness *(Ps. 103)*. Prayer is a petition for personal help.

David, in *Psalm 51*, shows his grief and remorse after his affair with Bathsheba. To even the strong Christian who seeks to be delivered from guilt, *John 4:24 (NKJV)* says,

> God is a spirit and those who worship him must worship in spirit and in truth.

> Or do you not know that your body is the temple of the Holy Spirit who is in you, who you have from God, and are not your own? For you were bought with a price: Therefore glorify God in your body, and in your spirit, which are Gods. *(1 Cor. 6:19–20, NKJV)*

Jesus prayed in times of decision and crisis:

- During His baptism *(Luke 3:21–22)*
- Before choosing the twelve disciples *(Luke 6:12–13)*
- During His transfiguration *(Luke 9:29)*
- Throughout His ministry, in sustained service *(Mark 1:35–39)*
- Before raising Lazarus from the dead *(John 11:41–42)*
- As a result of His burden for Peter *(Luke 22:31–32)*
- When facing His betrayal, abandonment, and execution *(Mark 14:32–42)*
- Concerning His disciples' future ministry *(John 17)*
- Prior to and during His death on the cross *(Luke 23:46)*

Also in times of joy:

- Rejoicing in His disciples' understanding *(Luke 10:21)*
- During the Last Supper *(Luke 22:17)*

What are the basics of prayer? First, we must accept Jesus Christ as our Savior and Lord. Second, we must understand the term *avail*, which simply means presenting ourselves to be of use, to assist, and to serve.

Prayer MUST BE

1. made in faith. Trust in the Lord that your prayer is heard and will be answered *(Heb. 11:6, Matt. 17:20, Mark 11:23–24, James 1:6)*;
2. made in the name of Jesus Christ, not just with thoughtless words *(John 14:13, 15:16)*;
3. made in keeping and asking for the will of God. Do not be egocentric *(1 John 5:14–15)*;
4. made under the direction of the Holy Spirit *(Matt. 20:22, John 4:10, Rom. 8:26–27)*;

5. made by one who has confessed and renounced sin *(Ps. 66:18, Prov. 28:9, Isa. 59:1–2)*;

6. made with a forgiving heart—the lack of forgiveness is a fatal hindrance to effective intercession *(Matt. 6:12–15, 18:21–35; Mark 11:25–26; James 5:14–16)*;

7. made in the context of a harmonious relationship on the human level *(Matt. 5:23–24, 18:19; 1 Pet. 3:1–7)*;

8. made with importunity or persistence of genuine care, compassion, and concern *(Luke 11:5–8, 18:1–8)*

9. made with concentration and intensity *(James 5:16)*.

With all those *must be*s, we must remember the power of prayer. God answers prayer but not usually as quickly as we want. Remember, His answers are *yes, no,* and *wait.*

Didn't I just say God answers prayers? God knows our needs better than we do ourselves, and His answer may be *no.* For example, we may ask to be monetarily wealthy. Job essentially asked, "What profit should we have if we pray unto Him?" It is an incalculable profit. Prayer is the major working of God in our lives and the source of vision, power, creativity, and blessings in personal experiences. It definitely deserves our highest priority *(Luke 18:1, Eph. 6:18, Phil. 4:6, 1 Tim. 2:1, 1 Thess. 5:17)*. If we neglect prayer, it is a sin because it stops God's grace in our lives. Our lives should be one long-running conversation with the Father. Paul prayed "unceasingly" for the churches he visited.

> For God whom I serve in my spirit in the preaching of the gospel of His Son is my witness as to how unceasingly I make mention of you always in my prayers, making request, if perhaps now at last by the will of God, I may succeed in coming to you. *(Rom. 1:9–10, AMP)*

> With all prayers and petition pray…at all times…in the Spirit, and with this in view stay

alert with all perseverance and petition…for all God's people. *(Eph. 6:18, AMP)*

We give thanks to God the Father our Lord Jesus Christ praying always for you. *(Col. 1:3, KJV)*

We give thanks to God always for all of you, making mention of you in our prayers. *(1 Thess. 1:2, KJV)*

For this reason we also constantly thank God that when you received the word of God which you heard from us, you accepted it not as the word of men, but for what it really is, the word of God, which also performs its work in you who believe. *(1 Thess. 2:13, New American Standard Bible [NASB])*

And finally,

Pray without ceasing. *(1 Thess. 5:17, KJV)*

One last thought on prayer:

As I mentioned before, this is you-God time. *Wow!* What a glorious time! He gives us the opportunity to thank Him for all He has done for us every day. You can request from our God the help that you need. When you come to Him with a righteous heart and forgiving spirit, your night and the next day will go so much better.

Fellowship

Fellowship is the next Christian fundamental, as is being a strong teammate. What is fellowship? Think of the great times you have had at practice, to and from games, and during the games. As a head coach, I had monthly Saturday breakfasts with the captain and possibly the seniors as well. It was at those times, in a relaxed, enjoyable atmosphere, that we would discuss issues and potential problems. I had a twofold purpose. One was to give them a true role of leadership in the team. The second was to listen to issues I may not have been aware of.

If you are a coach, I hope you don't think you have all the answers. Use your team leaders as an effective resource. Being on the same page is important for both of you. Also, it is a great time to fellowship with your leaders.

When I was at Riverside High School in Painesville, Ohio, I observed many of our athletes having their own pregame meal at Chick-fil-A. Right after school, they would head off for nourishment, both physical and emotional. They grew more and more together. As the year progressed, I would see them invite the younger players.

This tradition started to be passed on. They grew equally close together in that setting, as they did in practice and games. Bus rides are sometimes considered forced fellowship; but this, too, is a great opportunity to grow. Some coaches demand quiet time while traveling to the event. If that be the case, then allow fellowship on the return trip.

Our Savior truly believed in fellowship, not only with His disciples but in many instances shown in the Bible:

- At the wedding at Cana Jesus attended, where He performed His first miracle *(John 2:1–11)*.
- During His teachings to the multitudes at the Sermon on the Mount *(Matt. 5:1–16)*.
- With the many thousands who followed Him, like Mary and Martha and Lazarus or in the home of Simon Peter's mother-in-law *(Luke 10:38–44, Matt. 8:14–15)*.
- At the Passover meal in the upper room, where He showed His love for His disciples by demonstrating how to be a servant in *John 13:1–17*.

We must fellowship with other Christians, our teammates, if we are to continue our training regimen. Being a faithful church-goer is a basic for us. It is a basic fundamental. We know how it is being around our teammates. Well, these are our teammates on God's team. There are times, as an athlete or coach, when attending certain services or church functions is impossible; but Sunday morning is a *must*.

Yes, it is important to listen to the Word of God during a service, but the time you spend before and after church is equally important. Think of the opportunities to share with others their joys and sorrows. Think of how you can be the one that encourages your brother or sister in Christ in time of stress or turmoil. This builds and encourages our walk with the Lord.

If you ain't progressing, you are regressing. If church attendance doesn't become a strong possibility for you, then look for other opportunities to fellowship. As a coach, it may be with faculty members at lunch. For a student, lunchtime and before classes begin. All offer numerous opportunities. If time or opportunities still don't avail themselves, remember your other fundamentals.

Reading His Word

Studying and reading the Bible, the Word of God, is something you can always make time for. I suggest a good solid Bible translation that you can understand. Some may not deal well with the *thee*s and *thou*s in the King James Version. You may want to search for a more understandable version. There are many good translations available.

A good daily devotional book can be a fantastic way to either start or end your day. Reading the Word is like any other fundamental; the more you do it, the better you get and the easier it becomes. The more time you spend in the Word, the more you will start looking forward to your time in the Word. You may start your day with the Word to get energized or end your day with it to give you peace and answers for the issues and problems of that day.

As we think about becoming a champion athlete, we must always remember who blessed us with our skills and abilities: our Lord and Savior. You work hard daily to become the best you can be, but remember that you are made in His image.

Glorify God in all you do. Why can't we use this daily work on fundamentals to improve our walk with God? Guess what? We can! Pray unceasingly, fellowship, not only hear but listen to people, bring God's Word to those who are hurting, and get into His Word—daily reading!

Service

You must work on service. You might be saying, "But I am just a young man or woman, how can I serve? All the adults seem to take the important roles."

Do you like working with young kids? Go help in a Sunday school class. I'm sure the teacher would be very thankful for the help. Maybe you have some wheelchair-bound church members. Go help them. What skill and ability has God given you? Can you read well? See if you can go to a nursing home and read to people. I think you will realize how good it feels when you help someone. That is service.

Are you strong, artistic, a good listener? Think of how the Lord has blessed you. In the summer, can you help at vacation Bible school? Maybe you could work at a Christian summer camp. Sometimes, it may be a community project asking for helpers.

When you come with a strong foundation in Christ, the people around you will see Him through you. Service is something that may require a little research or observation, but there are many ways to serve the Lord. Feed, clothe, listen, and help. Our Lord and Savior in the upper room showed Himself to be a servant as He took the time to wash the feet of His disciples. When done with a humble heart and spirit, service glorifies the Lord.

2

Being a Good Teammate

I relate this chapter of being a good teammate to being a good member of your church. What does it take to be a good teammate?

- Being one who all members can trust in and have faith in to do the expected job.
- Being one who places the needs of others ahead of his own.
- Being one who is always positive in the face of adversity.
- Being one who is a leader, one that others will follow into battle.

In the church sense, it can best be summed up as reliable. Can you do the work you are asked to do without having to have the spotlight shine on you? The only light that needs to shine is God's light shining in and from us as we go about our daily lives.

A good teammate does the job regardless of how menial the task may seem. That teammate doesn't seek the headlines, such as scoring great numbers of points or having great stats. What he does is make things possible without great fanfare. He practices daily humbleness and humility. His concern is the result. Does your church body have a need? Can you use the skills and abilities you may have to meet that need?

Simply put, be worthy of your teammates' trust. Be trustworthy. Be the servant; be self-sacrificing. Be the one who lifts up a teammate who just made a mistake. In your church, are you the one who lifts up the person that made the mistake/error in judgment or the person that you can see by their body language is just in need of a friend?

Do members trust you? Daily be the light of encouragement and hope. Do you do this in your workplace? Are people drawn to you? Be a great teammate at work. Jesus becomes our guide to becoming a great teammate. By His service to His disciples, His service and healing of the sick, blind, and lame. He served His people *(Matt. 20:26–28)*. The Son of God did not come to be served but to serve. Think about how His walk upon this earth guided us to live and how His death upon the cross took our sins away. Do you want to be a good teammate? Do you want to be Christlike in your walk? Put God first.

A good teammate is an encourager. No one is perfect during the heat of the game. With the pressure of a deadline, mistakes occur. No coach is perfect. No boss is perfect. Jesus was the only perfect one to walk this earth two thousand years ago. In other words, when a teammate or coworker makes a mistake, be the encourager that tells them it is okay, we will get the next one. At work, telling them it will get worked out. The person who made the mistake feels bad enough and doesn't need someone compounding the error. But a good shot of encouragement is another way of saying, "We're all in this together."

Invite that troubled one to come along with you. Show him your walk, walk with him, and show him the path you have chosen. The Bible says in *Matthew 25:35–36*, "For I was hungry and you gave Me food; I was thirsty and you gave Me drink; I was a stranger and you took Me in; I was naked and you clothed Me; I was sick and you visited Me; I was in prison and you came to Me." When you feed the hungry, when you clothe the naked, when you help your fellow man, when you help the least, these gifts are equivalent to giving to God.

A good teammate uses his heart, not just his head, when dealing with mistakes and errors. Give a pat on the back, a handshake, and some uplifting words. If you become upset with a situation, that's when Satan can easily step in. Be strong and don't allow him to come in. Be the leader on the floor, field, work, or church. Your actions become the sign of being a great teammate. Be the one who shows Christ through your actions at all times. Yes, you want to be successful. That is one of the reasons you are out there. More important is glorifying God in all you do. Be the *light* Jesus wants you to be.

3

How Can I Be a Better Coach?

I know there are thousands of books out there regarding the *X*s and *O*s of coaching. I put many of them on my bookshelf thinking they held the key to winning the state championship. No, I did not find the key. However, my years of experience have taught me more than any book. Much more of your team success is based on your players, not on a new out-of-bounds play or a new defensive scheme. Thus, my thought process has changed from looking for the magic button to push to more introspection and to learning how I can better reach my players.

Don't get me wrong. I believe that a coach must stay up on all areas and new thoughts of the game. I still attend clinics and subscribe to current magazines. I still talk and exhibit my passion for coaching with other coaches. Plato said, "The first and best victory is to conquer self." That is to "know thyself."

The first question I would ask is, why do you coach? Is it a love of the game or sport? Do you have a passion for the sport? Is it for the money? Is it for your own ego? What is it that drives you?

First of all, if it is for the money, we need to talk. The hours worked versus pay does not even work out to minimum wage level. If it does go above minimum wage, then you may be cheating your athletes. The ability to coach and direct young athletes today is a blessing from God. As a Christian coach, however, a love for God must be your number one priority. Is your passion for the Lord greater than your passion for your sport?

Your players participate in that sport for many reasons: a love of the game, a great ability to play the game, because their friends are playing, or because of a newfound interest. Whatever the reason may be, they are in your charge. What you do with that charge will have some impact, great or small, on their lives. As a coach, I want to impart to those athletes the love and passion for the game. More important is that they see my walk with Christ on a daily basis.

I have heard and read that a team takes on the personality of their coach. I do find that to be true. Think about how you are at practice. Do you exhibit enthusiasm and knowledge of the game? Do you teach to a level of understanding? Think about our Lord and Savior. He taught in parables and used the current everyday surroundings to get His point across. Is that you?

Today's society says our kids are different. They want instantaneous results. They are entitled to playing time just because they are out for the team and many other so-called differences. Some of those things are true to some extent, but if the members of the team are dedicated to do their best, then those things of today become minor concerns.

One rule we have made is no cell phones out of the locker room. It seems simple enough, but we coaches realize their connections have become addictive. Focus at practice is crucial. As a coach, you must lead with that example.

How does this relate to our love of God? It is important that our athletes see us as a man or woman of God. This does not just happen on the court or field. Many of you are also teachers. Do your athletes see the same work out of you in the classroom in dealing with colleagues, administrators, or parents? There must be consistency in your walk. Many are watching you and seeing what you do. What we do is more important than what we say. Your walk is constant; and your daily fundamentals of prayer, Bible reading, service, and fellowship go a long way in strengthening you for your daily walk in the world of coaching.

How do you deal with other coaches? Are you known as a role model for your athletes? Do other coaches ask you about how your team shows such great sportsmanship but plays to their utmost?

Sometimes it is difficult because some others in the coaching rank may hold to the thought that winning at all costs is the only goal. Believe me, I've known a few of those in my day.

Sometimes the competitiveness we have may fall to that level. I think about the apostle Paul and how he frequently made references to racing and the prize. All along, the prize was in the effort and what was done to get to the finish line. The prize awaiting us on this earth is peace beyond understanding in our daily walk. Also awaiting is *ruling and reigning* with Jesus in eternity.

> If we suffer, we shall also reign with him: if we deny him, he also will deny us. *(2 Tim. 2:12, KJV)*

> And hast made us unto our God kings and priests: and we shall reign on the earth. *(Rev. 5:10, KJV)*

Are you driven by goals? One, do you know what you want and how to get it? I always set high team goals, conference champs, sectional, district, regional, and state champs. Two, do you have individual goals, such as head a Fellowship of Christian Athletes group, lead people to Christ, or maybe stay healthy all year? These can help you and further the walk you are called to do. Modeling Christ's walk in the halls and on the court or field is a goal that will help you to reach others.

Don't assume that your team members all have the same goals as you. We have found that early season goal setting helps in understanding the athlete and also gives you a chance to focus on misdirected goals. I have already mentioned our Saturday morning captain's breakfast. This has been a great help in establishing and focusing on team stuff.

Living a healthy life is crucial. The long hours coaches put in require a discipline for healthy living. What good is it for you and your team if you are sick? I know our season frequently went twenty to twenty-one weeks. That requires a long time to focus and do the right things. It is difficult to focus either at practice or a game if you are not well. Thus, you maybe cheating your program and not glorifying God in your work. Remember, He has placed you in an important position. Honor Him by staying healthy.

A great godly leader is always placing the needs of others ahead of themselves. I think we do this almost naturally, based upon our position. The more you show you care, the better your coaching will become. Be in tune with your players. As a coach, I like to be first on the court and see every athlete as they come on the field or court. If you see trouble on their face, mention it, but call them in after practice to talk. Make sure you do! In order to get athletes to open up, a level of trust and knowing that you care must be established. Don't give lip service to your athletes because they will know. Pray every day for the ability to see issues and problems and that you will be made aware of them.

Be a positive, consistent influence in the lives of your athletes. That attitude builds up confidence, and confidence makes for better players. When it comes down to crunch time, that confidence builds success.

Game Preparation

A coach must prepare his/her charges for the next game, games, or season. The plan must include daily fundamentals and knowledge of the strengths and weaknesses of potential opponents. Long-range planning must include an understanding of your own philosophy, your assessment of available talent, and what to expect from the opponent.

In the long-range planning, a master practice plan should be complete. The plan should include your goals and how you and your athletes are going to reach them. I break down plans into three segments: preseason regimens, regular regimens, and tournament tune-up. As new Christians begin their walk, it can be broken down into three segments as well: discovering Christ in their life, sticking with the fundamentals, and becoming more and more of a mature Christian.

Our preseason plan is geared toward our first game, hard work on fundamentals, and putting the pieces together for that game. In the same way, a new Christian finds out what works and what doesn't. Establish the habit of prayer and Bible reading. You as a coach must understand your philosophy and constantly assess your players' abilities. Looking at the skills and abilities of your players is crucial when coaching. When Jesus chose His team, He chose from a variety of personalities and professions. From fishermen to a tax collector (a most hated man), young and old mature men. What a great mix.

In public schools, you often don't get to choose who you want. The stronger your program becomes, the younger athletes will understand and learn from your veterans how things need to be done. My thoughts turn to Jesus and the teachings He brought to His disciples before He sent them on their first missions. He equipped them, He trained them, and with instructions, He sent them *(Matt. 9:36–10:42)*. Do you equip, train, and send your athletes out to do battle?

In our Christian walk, what does Satan try to do? From the fall of man in the garden of Eden to the present day, Satan wants to see failure. He wants, through deceptions and lies, to steal the greatness God has for you.

Drugs are a part of what athletes have to face in our society today. That deception to attempt to bolster performances with the use of anabolic steroids and other drugs has worked its way from the professional ranks down to high schools. False teachers are telling your athletes that they are or can be something they are not. Satan doesn't want to see success based upon Christian values of glorifying God in their work ethic. Satan says, "Take the easy way," not showing the posted warning signs along the way.

As a leader (coach), we must be aware of the potential problems Satan can and will bring to your team. Sometimes it's jealousy, trying to create division. Sometimes it's the breaking of your training rules. Sometimes it's the dislike of teammates by other teammates. There can be many attacks against your team strengths. Daily be aware of potential problems. Don't allow Satan to get a foothold on your team. Remember, Satan is only full of lies.

As we prepare for battle (game), we have the confidence in our preparations, abilities, and game plan. I know all games are important; but sometimes they may seem bigger. If you are a huge underdog, sticking to fundamentals will put lots of pressure on the heavily favored team. You get a lead, and all of the sudden, the pressure upon them switches.

The same can be said when we face an extremely difficult situation in life. We are the underdogs, and Satan loves it. Concentrate even more on your fundamentals of prayer, reading the Word, service, and fellowship. Fill up your vessel with Godly things. I'm not saying all problems will go away, but you will be able to handle the situation much better. If you are heavily favored, it's sometimes difficult to maintain concentration. I used to motivate my tennis players with Dairy Queen Blizzard coupons if they maintained their concentration and defeated their opponent 6–0, 6–0.

This also relates to our walk. When things are going well, do you still pray, read the Word of God, fellowship, and be a servant? Thank the Lord for His blessings. As a coach, you must show confidence and a positive attitude even in difficult circumstances. What do athletes see in you? They look to their coach as a leader. You are given that awesome responsibility and have many opportunities to influence your athletes. Follow your plans and goals, prioritize. All coaches are pressed for time.

For those of you who teach in a classroom and coach, I know it seems that you are always a day behind (at least). I have seen new coaches be influenced by the latest trend. Having not yet developed their own philosophy, they may be swayed by it. It is important to *know yourself.* When things aren't going well on a scheduled ten-minute drill, do you stay on that drill or move onto the next? Remember, your athletes will read you and feel your stress and frustration. *Move on!* The more disciplined you are, the more your athletes will notice and the more disciplined they will become.

Patience is crucial to coaching. Some of us are type A personalities and want things done *yesterday.* Patience and hard work go well with a positive attitude. Think about how much love our God has for us and how patient He is with us. I for one am certainly glad for our Lord's love and patience.

Make no excuses. There will be hurdles to conquer, but we can do all things through Christ, who strengthens us. Some of those hurdles come not only in coaching but in relationships, life, and our walk with God. Sometimes a starter is injured the day before a big game. Sometimes coaches use this as an excuse for losing. Instead, look at this as an opportunity to use your strength and influence to bring the team even closer together. Will the replacement step up? Be encouraging, and stress to your team the positive attitude. Your team will be looking at you to see how you handle adversity.

At times, your significant other will disappoint you, and it may cause your anger to rise. That is the devil trying to step in and influence and divide. Don't get off the path of righteousness. Satan wants that to happen. Get more into God's Word, and prayer will drive Satan behind you. God will *not forsake you*. Stay focused and don't allow Satan's distractions to sway you.

I've known many great coaches who have never won state championships. In fact, in Ohio basketball, the only team that won their final game is the team that won the state championship. As I previously stated, coaches set their goals to win the state championship. Coaches focus and start their seasons by doing all they can to prepare and work toward that goal. They are focusing on their reward.

As a coach, we push and train our athletes to be their best. Is it hard? Will you meet resistance? Will it be frustrating at times? *Yes!* Your athletes must be convinced that doing things the right way is the goal. Pay attention to details, and the big things will take care of themselves. Sometimes we get caught up in the big picture and forget what it takes to plug in the pieces so that the big picture will be clear. Sometimes these big pictures take time to develop. This is where patience comes to the forefront. Shortcuts to success don't create good quality work.

What is our reward? Life eternally with our Lord and Savior, walking on the streets of gold, and singing His praises. There are times when we slip off the path of righteousness, but keep in mind that Christ died for our sins. Go to God in prayer, cleanse your heart, and ask for His forgiveness. Life upon the path of righteousness is so much smoother. Hurdles do show up once in a while, but maintain your focus on the prize, the goal—our eternal life. Continue on life's journey with total confidence in your future.

For example, for three and a half years, I worked with one of our past players to bring her to her fullest God-given abilities. Then one day in practice in her senior year, I was guarding her when she made the move we had been working on. I went crazy, in a good way, then took the ball and bounced it twenty-five to thirty feet in the air, saying, "*Yes!*" (It got stuck behind part of our wall heater.) She reached the goal we had been working toward.

Side note: the next year, I saw her make the same move in the NCAA tournament against Purdue. I smiled and said, "I've seen that move before."

4

Discipline of God

The basis for this chapter comes from *Hebrews 12,* which follows the thought of the Christian race and walk. Some consider life's path to be a marathon. Having run marathons, I know you don't go out and start your training with a twenty-mile run. However, in order to run a marathon, one must start with easy short runs and then build up. Much like a new Christian cannot just jump in and start preaching and teaching, marathon training takes time. It will also take time to build up your faith. When we plan our running, we know that it will take lots of hard work, but the rewards will be great. The same holds true in our life's walk. We know there will be hardship and difficulties, but we also know the rewards will be great.

There are common attributes to reach those great rewards, both in training for a marathon and our life walk. Endurance is obviously needed for a marathon. Staying on the path of righteousness also requires endurance. Passion is another quality for a marathon runner. You are not going to be denied. Aches, pains, and little injuries will not stop you from achieving your goal. These times of overcoming make you stronger because you know what you have endured to reach your goal. *Hebrews 12* also brings to light how life's difficulties can sometimes set us back. But when we keep our focus on Jesus and the reward He promises, we know we can make it through. Getting through difficulties with Christ as our guide builds up our endurance for the next problem that might occur. When we remember what Christ went through for us, our difficulties seem trivial.

There are times when the Lord sees us falling off the righteous path, and He chastens us. When we are corrected by the Lord, it is for our own good. If God did not love us, He would not chasten us. Have we ever been corrected by our earthly father, sent to time-out, grounded, or spanked with the yardstick or spoon? Sure we have, and when we look back, we deserved it. We need correction in our life, and our heavenly Father only wants what is best for us. Accept it, grow from it, and then return to the path God wants us to walk on.

What is our purpose in running the race? Is it good conditioning? Is it the challenge of 26.2 miles? What would it be? The purpose of our race in life is to reach our goal of spending eternity on the glorious streets of heaven. We look to those who have gone on before us to lead us to that victory—our Lord and Savior and the saints who have paved the way. Now it is *our* race. We now enter the starting blocks and focus on the commands. In elementary school it was "Ready, set, go!" In high school track, it's "Runners, take your mark, set." *Bang!* The gun goes off. As we are getting set, we sometimes look to the right and left, sizing up our competition. That's a wrong move. Focus on what you need to do. Thoughts creep in: "I have prepared well, my training, my lifting, running mile after mile, running hills (my personal obstacle), eating properly, and resting, knowing that I want to be the one who gives my best effort."

As one who wants to improve my walk with God, I attempt to glorify God in all I do.

- My lifting consists of lifting praises to our Lord and Savior.
- My endurance training is done by increasing my Bible reading and prayer.

You must conquer obstacles you may face every day. People say things to you, such as "Are you one of those God guys?" Maybe a handsome man or beautiful woman passes by and some lustful thoughts creep in. Did you find a large sum of money? Did someone cut you off while you were driving? Maybe an ad or magazine at the checkout counter caught your eye.

The obstacles are around us daily, and our strength is challenged. Satan has many ways to attack weaker minds and bodies. But walking with our Lord on His path is always our choice. It's not that we want those tests and temptations, but we know that we must be prepared to face them. Satan doesn't want us to run along that straight path. He doesn't want us to reach the finish line.

Our training plan consists of the following:

- *Proper diet (daily Bible reading).* Are you taking in enough of God's Word? An undernourished or improperly nourished body is not going to win any race.
- *Prayer life.* Is our daily routine one of communing with God, who is our trainer, and listening to His words thus giving us strength for the day?
- *Rest.* The aspect of rest doesn't always seem to fit well into certain personality types. But to me, resting in the arms of our Lord and Savior gives me peace and comfort. On the seventh day of creation, God rested. In so doing, He gave us a day to keep holy by pulling away from the issues of the week, sharing with other believers the love of our Lord, and sharing both the good and bad things of the week. Basically, we are enjoying the love of our Lord as expressed from those we see and hear.

Self-Discipline

All great athletes and many good ones exercise self-discipline. The hard, totally committed work it takes to be great in your field requires great self-discipline. Just imagine if everyone on your team or in your workplace would work to the glory of God. What a fantastic team and workplace you would have.

Self-discipline requires passion, and passion leads to endurance. The driving force between being mediocre and great is the passion you have. Some just want to stay in their comfort zone and not venture out beyond that. What is holding you back? Is it internal or external? If it is internal, remind yourself that the Holy Spirit is inside you, and drive Satan's attempt over you away. If it is external, look to the Lord in prayer to give you the strength to step out and experience what God has for you.

How disciplined are you? Are you like Esau, who, for a morsel of food, sold his birthright to satisfy his earthly hunger? "And Jacob said, Sell me this day thy birthright. And Esau said, Behold, I am at the point to die: and what profit shall this birthright do to me? And Jacob said, Swear to me this day; and he sware unto him: and he sold his birthright unto Jacob" *(Gen. 25:31–33, KJV)*.

Are you willing or tempted to sell your given inheritance for a moment's pleasure? We are all children of God and inheritors of the kingdom. Christian self-discipline is or may be required at every corner we turn.

Athletes consistently strive for perfection in their sport, be it never missing a shot or a block, a putt inside 10 feet, or a perfect 10 on the balance beam. Whatever that striving might be, should ours be any less when we are striving for eternal peace with our Savior in the eternal home He has waiting for us? Turn to the Lord to find the peace and comfort He promises.

When we make that commitment to the Lord, what are our expectations? If we are lukewarm and not fully giving of ourselves, not accepting the chastening of the Lord and correcting our behavior, we shall be as the beast touching the holy mountain, stoned or killed with an arrow. Moses trembled and feared what God would do.

> When Moses saw it, he wondered at the sight: and as he drew near to behold it, the voice of the Lord came unto him, Saying, I am the God of thy fathers, the God of Abraham, and the God of Isaac, and the God of Jacob. Then Moses trembled, and durst not behold. Then said the Lord to him, Put off thy shoes from thy feet: for the place where thou standest is holy ground. *(Acts 7:31–33, KJV)*

But we come to Mount Zion and the city of our living God, the heavenly Jerusalem. We look forward to being with the angels, committed Christians, God our judge, spirits of perfect men, with Jesus our mediator, His blood sprinkling upon us, washing away our sins. When we face trials and temptations, it is God alive in us that gives us confidence to stay the course, for we know the temporal rewards in this earth are nothing compared to what awaits us in His holy kingdom. Can we or will we receive His kingdom that cannot be shaken? Let us show gratitude by which we offer to God an acceptable service with reverence and awe.

5

Ben Franklin and the Vessel

In *Poor Richard's Almanac*, there's a well-known saying: "Early to bed, early to rise, makes a man healthy, wealthy, and wise."

My thoughts on this topic were inspired by my pastor's wife while talking about filling our bodies, which are God's temple, where He resides within us. "What? know ye not that your body is the temple of the Holy Ghost which is in you, which ye have of God, and ye are not your own" *(1 Cor. 6:19)*? She was talking about filling our bodies with God stuff. She didn't say 98 percent or 99 percent. She said 100 percent. If we do that, Satan doesn't have a chance to squeeze in there. However, if we leave that 1 percent or 2 percent opening, he will take that opportunity and bring self-doubt, shame, or ugly thoughts. We've been given three *g* words to help fill that space: goodness, godliness, and greatness. God desires greatness for us.

First, we need to go back to *Poor Richard*. "Early to bed, early to rise" is part of what we need to do. As an athlete, can you perform well on a few hours' sleep? You probably can't. If you follow that as a pattern for weeks at a time, you are not going to practice well. It comes down to your willingness to sacrifice for your good and thus the team's good. I understand, from those who have studied high school students, that they are frequently found to be nocturnal. It may be difficult to change these habits, but for yours and the team's good, it's worth the change.

I speak also to those who are attempting to improve your walk with Christ. In order to concentrate well and be what God wants you

41

to be, you must also take care of your body. Rest for you is recuperative, and the benefits are great. This enables you to study the Word better and to do God's work to the fullest. I know and realize that with adults, some things simply can't be avoided. When we prioritize things correctly, with God first, we will find things go much better.

Eating healthy is also important. A good, solid, nourishing diet gives you the energy needed for the day. Athletes need more calories because of age and activity, but remember, their metabolism is racing. As we get older, it seems to slow down. However, some studies have said it is based upon lack of exercise and still eating the same amount. Thus, the pounds begin to add up. Now, maybe you feel there just simply isn't enough time to exercise. I say to you, find ten minutes for a solid stretching program to keep those aging muscles supple and loose. You will find yourself with fewer aches and pains.

As I mentioned in a previous chapter, you must have a passion for that. The benefits are great. Can you find time to walk? Walking helps to physically strengthen your heart. As you do that, you will find time to be able to study and pray with greater intensity. It is also a great time to meditate and praise our Lord.

Appreciate and treat God's temple with reverence, respect, and holiness. We must fill up this vessel with God stuff. The Holy Spirit is given to you to indwell you, to be a comforter and counselor. The Word of God is something you can read, study, meditate on, and even memorize. The more you fill your vessel with God's Word, the better you can sense and understand what the Holy Spirit is speaking to you.

How can I get into God's Word better?

1. *Read.* Sounds simple enough, but don't just look at the words. Don't just *see* the words. Reading God's Word isn't just quantity; it's based on quality. Sometimes, if you are reading from a King James Version, you may struggle. Find a version that works well for you and still follow the scriptures. There are several versions available that are easier to understand. A good Christian bookstore or your pastor can help.

2. *Meditation.* A good, quiet place provides you with a place to think about the passages you've selected to read that day. It also and opens up communication with God by minimizing distractions. The more you meditate, the greater your understanding will be.

3. *Study.* This is an intense form of meditation. The studying you do will help you to discover truths you never saw before.

4. *Apply.* Once you have established the habits of getting into God's Word, you must use it. God will reveal to you what He wants you to do. Obey God! That is always the best path to follow. Say *no* to self and *yes* to Him.

5. *Memorize scripture.* I have to say this is not something I do well. However, if you read and have a passion to do this, you can memorize His Word. This is similar to developing an athletic skill. As a coach, it takes a long time to correct a habit. You use your memory every day. Why not use it to memorize scripture? How much should you try at first? Take baby steps. One or two verses will help to get you started. Try some of these methods: flash cards; rewrite the passage, repeat it in the car, on a walk, or wherever you can; set goals, and when you reach them, reward yourself. Hold yourself to memorizing, and be accountable for learning God's Word. Then repeat! Repeat! Repeat *(Prov. 16:1–3)*! Commit to the Lord.

6

Snippets

The Warmth of the Son

As a runner and one who is an early riser, I enjoy my morning runs, especially when the sun is beginning to show itself. One morning in the spring, it was just such the case. I started to see while I was running the shadows of darkness being broken up by the bright sunlight. Although the shade seemed much cooler, running toward the sun gave me the thoughts of experiencing the warmth of the sun.

When darkness creeps in, and Satan is attempting to destroy my walk, I run toward the *Son*. He gives to us His warmth, comfort, and peace along our path. It is better to run in that warmth, but if it's not possible, then look toward the Son. He is always present to give us His warmth.

Expectations

Our expectations and God's expectations sometimes collide. The reason they may collide is because sometimes we short side ourselves. We get ourselves to the gate, but someone (Satan) tells us we can't go in because we aren't worthy. Our Lord wants to take us further. He wants us to enter His gates and accept His desire for us to be great. We may not know what greatness God has in store for us, but if we come to God in prayer and obey what He speaks to us, then

He will reveal His plans for us. We were created in His image. We need to raise our expectations of ourselves and continue to raise our prayers to the Lord and listen and obey His words for us.

Little and Large

Our Lord and Savior gave us many learning experiences through parables. One day, I was searching frantically for something important. It was so important that if I couldn't find it, some issues may have arisen. All I had to do was search more diligently. That's what I did, and found it under some papers. It reminded me of when issues or problems hit, causing worry. It's then we need to search diligently for Jesus. He will provide for us, as He always does. Do we come to God when life's simple problems occur? I believe the more we depend on God, the stronger our faith becomes. He will provide for our needs. In the coaching area, it has been said that if you take care of the small fundamentals, the big ones seem to take care of themselves. Build up your faith, and trust in the Lord in all things, *little or large*.

Mondays

Have you ever had problems getting started on Mondays? We got out of our routine with a couple of days off, a little more staying up, and a little more sleeping in. Now, I am not saying that we don't need that time because we do. What I am saying is that we shouldn't give up the time we spend with God. If anything, the more free time we have, the more time we have to pray, read, serve, or fellowship. Don't get out of or away from your walk with Jesus. Stay the course. Stay on the right path, His way, even if your daily routine has changed. Fill your daily vessel with God stuff.

Obey

Do we always use the gifts, the skills, the abilities God has given us? If the opportunity presents itself and you can help, do you? In churches around our country, many of the same people within the congregation do the needed work time after time. Listen to God, and listen to the leaders of the church. What are the needs? When we don't do what God calls us to do, someone else will have to do it, probably taking away from things that other person has to do and is called for. Make yourself aware of what needs to be done, and apply your skill to that need. It doesn't have to be only in the church but in your community, workplace, or wherever. Ask God for that awareness. Trust that He will give you the guidance. Simply *obey* His call!

One Winter Morning

One morning while going out to get my morning paper, I slipped and lost a little traction on a slight incline. That gave me this thought: it's often easy to see the steep hill we are attempting to climb. We prepare ourselves for great effort, but other times, the obstacle isn't so recognizable. When Satan attacks, sometimes it is blatant, and then it's easy to put our guard up. However, it's the hidden, not so noticeable, ones that ensnare us. They can gradually wear us down without us even realizing it. There are times we slip and fall and wonder how it happened. We must prepare ourselves daily for Satan's attacks. Strengthening our mind, body, and spirit will prepare us well to fight off those attempts to cause us to slip.

God's Indwelling

It is important to take care of our bodies. When Satan attacks, our mental strength may be there, but our physical strength may be lacking. We must daily take care of our bodies, the temple in which God, through the Holy Spirit, resides in us.

The Holy Spirit deserves the best place to indwell. Be godly in what you do and what you eat. Cleanliness, strength, and flexibility all become important. It becomes difficult to focus when the pain receptors are firing to your brain. I'm not saying focusing on God can't be done if you are weak or ill, but why not just take great care of the temple of God?

I realize that as an athlete, a coach, or parent, things get in the way of wellness. The priority of physical well-being can get pushed back. Once those missed days are passed through, it's impossible to make them up. Normally, working out for an hour isn't going to be made up the next day by working out for two hours. That probably won't help; in fact, it may hurt you physically.

Prioritize your life by placing God first, family second, job third, thereby giving the Holy Spirit a place in which to dwell.

I have a saying that has been placed in my classrooms. It simply, thoughtfully says,

"Life is a matter of choices,
But remember with every choice comes consequences.
Some good, some bad.
It is my hope your choice is Jesus,
And that is definitely a great choice."

ABCs

A—Bring *A*doration to our Lord and Savior.
B—*B*elieve Jesus is the Son of God and alive today.
C—Never *C*ease praising Him.
D—King David *D*anced and praised our Lord.
E—Come to *E*ternal life through Jesus Christ our Lord /
        *E*verything you have is from God.
F—Increase your *F*aith in the Lord daily.
G—*G*ive 100 percent of yourself to the Lord.
H—*H*onor His holy name.

I—*I*ncrease your prayer life gradually, and you will receive bountiful rewards.

J—*J*esus is the answer to all our problems.

K—Our Lord is *K*ing and ruler over everything.

L—*L*ove the Lord with all you have.

M—*M*agnify His holy name by doing your work in a godly way.

N—*N*ighttime is a peaceful time for you to be with God.

O—Our God is *O*mnipotent and all-powerful.

P—Throwaway your *P*ride; all you have are gifts from God.

Q—*Q*uestions you have about life are all answered by God.

R—*R*epent and be saved.

S—Our *S*alvation is guaranteed through the blood of Jesus.

T—*T*hrow off the things of this world, and focus on God.

U—*U*nderstanding is increased in your conversation with God.

V—Your *V*alor will increase as you fill your heart with His Word.

W—*W*orship and praise God. Fill your heart, mind, and soul with His Word.

X—If God *X*-rays your heart, what will He find?

Y—*Y*ou are a child of God destined for greatness.

Z—Worship the Lord with *Z*eal.

7

In Closing

As I conclude my part in the first book, I look back at the months of work and do not even consider the time spent to be work. I never was a prolific writer, but following the guidance of our heavenly Father, the pen just flowed. I thank Him daily for His guidance. It is my hope that these words will touch people as they have touched me. To the athlete, be the light that God wants you to be. Hopefully, your teammates will be attracted to you, and your walk will be a witness. To the coach, be the model your team can look to in times of crisis or in joy. As a leader of young men or women, you are given a great responsibility but also a blessing. To the casual or fanatic spectator, eyes and ears are watching you. Good sportsmanship, respect for the authorities, and encouraging words are all biblical. Practice those things when you attend the events. May the Lord bring His blessings to you, your family, and your friends.

8

Thoughts on 1, 2, and 3 John

1 John

I began writing this commentary on 1 John in November of 2014 while I was working in South Carolina, following my writing of *If You Want to Be a Better Christian, Then Train like a Champion*. I was moved by God to write these words. I am not a pastor or preacher even though I have spoken at several places in the Conneaut, Ohio, area. All I do is listen to God and put down into words what I believe He asks me to. This work does not include the passages but does include chapter and verse on which I wrote.

Chapter 1

Verse 1. John is reminding us of what he has seen, heard, and what he has handled. This gives us the idea that John's authority in his writing comes from his knowing and being with the Lord and Savior Jesus Christ.

Verse 2. Any doubt? Jesus made Himself present for those to see and hear His message. He proclaims eternal life because of what John has experienced.

Verse 3. John is asking that those who hear Him or read His Words fellowship with the Father and His Son, Jesus Christ.

Verse 4. John's words give us direction and complete joy to Him.

Conditions for Fellowship

Verse 5. The message that John heard from Jesus reminds us that God is light, and no darkness exists in Him at all.

Verse 6. We can't give lip service to say we have fellowship with Him and then walk in the darkness of the world. If this is what we are practicing, it is a lie, and therefore, we are not truthful.

Verse 7. If we walk in the light, then we follow our Lord and Savior. We can then fellowship with one another. If we find ourselves in sin, then we know that His precious blood cleanses us. What great thoughts!

These cannot be stated enough. Walk in His light, follow the path that Jesus leads us upon. Are we going to sin? Yes. But when we pray and ask for forgiveness, then we can have faith that our Savior's blood will cleanse us. Find the path, read the Word, love our brothers and sisters. We know the greatest *love sacrifice* that our Lord made for all of us. Can we be a servant? Can we give of our time?

Verse 8. Do we have sin within us? Do we think sinful thoughts? Yes! That is our nature. Whatever it may be—lust, revenge, greed, or a number of many things similar to these—we deceive ourselves if we say we have no sin. In arrogance or ignorance of our state, we may feel that because our actions show us to be a good man or woman, we are right with God. But our heart is not pure because it is being guided by the darkness of the world. So the Word of God warns us that we may not know ourselves if we think we are all right, and we need to look closer.

Verse 9. This verse deals with confessing our sins. Our Lord and Savior is faithful and righteous to forgive our sins. But like the adulteress who was forgiven by Jesus, His words to her were to go and sin *no more*! When we sin, we are unrighteous, and we need His cleansing. His blood washes us and makes us clean and righteous. What a thought to be righteous. Meaning, we are meeting the standards of what is right and just, morally right, and guiltless. What high standards our Lord sets for us. To be morally pure, to be righteous in all we do, not only in our actions but also in our thoughts and in our heart.

Verse 10. By saying or thinking that we have never sinned, we are lying to ourselves. Our Lord knows that we have sinned, and He died so our sins would be forgiven. Do we then make Jesus a liar? We all know that we have sinned, and if we say that we haven't, then we are still living in the darkness of the world. That is what the prince of darkness wants us to believe. "It wasn't a sin," so says Satan. The process of justifying what we do or have done doesn't make the sin any less sin in the eyes of God. Ask for forgiveness and sin *no more*.

Chapter 2

Verse 1. I see John writing this verse to new Christians who are frequently referred to as children. New Christians may not understand John asking them not to sin. Even if they do knowingly sin, John uses the term *advocate*, referring to Jesus, who is present before the throne of God as a totally righteous intercessor.

Jesus has given to us on earth the Holy Spirit, who is present to help us turn away from sin and turn to the righteous way of life. This is done without question and with total love. (*John's* gospel *14:16:* "And I will ask the Father, and he will give you another advocate to help you and be with you forever.")

Verse 2. The only satisfaction that meets our sins is God's Son, Jesus Christ. It is not just for us but for the entire world. What a statement! Because John knew and realized that all people could be saved. It is so important to get the *good news* out to the whole world so that the righteous path can be followed. Jesus is the advocate and God's gift for the remission of our sins. Do people ever think and worry that they have been sinning? If not, it is our role to tell them or just to say that there is a better way. That way is to follow the light to Jesus and to follow His light throughout our life.

Verse 3. John tells us that if we want to know Him, we must obey His commandments. This may seem to be a simple statement, but Jesus said, "Love your God with all your heart, soul, and mind. The second [commandment] is similar, Love your neighbor." Obedience to His commandments is the beginning. The more we follow His words, the easier it becomes. It is like establishing a habit. That habit is based upon loving both God and your neighbor.

Verse 4. To me the key thought in this verse is found in the beginning. Does the one who says "I have come to know Him" give only lip service to and about the Lord? I know and realize that once the words roll off our tongue, they are out there for all to hear. But the question is, where did those words come from? Do our words cause people to think that they are coming from our heart, or do they seem to be words of deception? I guess there are varying degrees. Do we say these things so that others may hear us and thus become prideful in our hearts? Or are our words pure and true delivered from our heart? The second part of this verse asks us if we are keeping His commandments. If not, then we are liars, and the truth does not exist in our heart. We must not only be cognizant of what we say but also of the source of our words.

Verse 5. Do we want to be in Christ? If so, we must keep our word. I look at this verse in a couple of ways. One says we must keep our word. Meaning, our yes is yes, and our no is no. The old thought of our words being good today is frequently gone by the wayside. We often hear politicians and others put a spin on their words so that they will be more acceptable to the public. But where is the honest and true man? It is a man of his word.

The second thought is the keeping of the Word of the Lord. This is *more* critical for the Christian if his desire is to be in Christ. The keeping of the Word yes, but we must know it and study it. Then *keep* it. When this happens, the love of God will fill us.

Verse 6. Do we live in Christ? If we do, it becomes paramount that we learn His walk. To follow in the footsteps of Christ, we must study, ingest, and encompass His Word. It sometimes becomes a magical kind of thinking when we visualize Christ walking through the Holy Land. We imagine that we are listening to His teachings or wondering at the meaning of His parables. Reading over and over again and attempting to understand our Lord and Savior's desire for us. Is it a narrow path, a slippery path, or a flat smooth road? When our thoughts come to this verse, it will hopefully cause us to want to study His life upon the earth. Yes, the Old Testament sets the stage for us; but the New Testament gives us hope, light, and confidence in our future.

Verse 7. John brings us the thoughts of His Word, who was present from the beginning. When He brings to us the light, the darkness goes away. The dawning of a new day happens within us when we bring Jesus Christ into our lives. His light suppresses the darkness, that is, any darkness which may still be a part of our lives. Gone is despair, loneliness, and all terrible feelings which are part of darkness. This is what happens when we let the light of Jesus Christ shine through us.

Verse 8. Hatred cannot be part of our makeup. Forgiveness and love toward our brothers and sisters is often difficult when we think that we have been wronged. But our thoughts need to turn to our Lord and Savior, who, even though He was without sin, was taken to the cross for our sins. How then can we not forgive those who may have wronged us?

Have you ever held on to anger and hatred toward someone? You may not even notice how that eats at your light. It will nibble away bite by bite until you are totally consumed by darkness. Forgive that one, and bring the light back into your being. As we know, the longer we hold on to ill feelings toward another, the more it eats at your light. *Again, forgive!*

Verse 10. Love with the total light within you. Allow the love and the light of our Lord and Savior to shine through for all to see at all times. Stumbling can be caused by a lack of love in the body. Are we totally full of His light? Do we put into practice the love that He has shined on us to all people, not just our friends but our enemies too?

Verse 12. What a simple and powerful statement it is that our sins are forgiven for His name's sake. The newest Christian can *know* that his sins are forgiven. Think about it, bring up the name of Jesus, ask for forgiveness, and truly believe. Then we are forgiven, and once forgiven, "go and sin no more."

Can we do the same? Can we forgive someone who has sinned against us or wronged us in any way? Follow the teachings of His Word and *forgive*. If we do, we are blessed, and the burdens of hatred and revenge are gone.

Verse 13–14. This verse encompasses all people no matter how long they have walked with the Lord, whether spiritual fathers, and/ or spiritual children. To the fathers, because of their experience in the Word, they have become mature in the faith. They know the Word well. The young men addressed here are strong. Does this mean physical or emotional strength? I can see this meaning both.

Physical strength can give one the endurance to stay in the Word and the ability to fight off the forces of evil when necessary. Emotionally, the young men who have received the Word may be on fire for the Lord, and that youthful enthusiasm is seen and appreciated. On the other hand, this verse can refer to all, regardless of age, who are well-versed in the Word and the life of Christ. The children mentioned in verse 14 is referring to newer Christians compared to the spiritual fathers.

Verses 15–17. The thoughts of these three verses refer to the focus of our love. It needs to be not toward the world. The world only gives lustful desires (both sexual and for the unsatisfied yearnings for possessions) and boasting pride. These are so ungodly and lead to darkness. When that occurs, the love of God is extinguished from our heart, and darkness enters in. We must remember that the world is passing away, and with it, what we lust for and have pride in will also be gone. What will be left? When we follow and abide in God's will, we shall be with Him for eternity.

Verse 18. John is writing here to warn us of the spirit of antichrist. Since this is the last hour, we need to be aware. As those of us in this century frequently look for signs of the end times and the coming of *the* Antichrist, we wonder who, when, and where. We must remember all of this is God's time and plan. An interpretation of this verse also refers to many persons being the antichrist (lowercase *a*), but these people are those who speak out in denial and in actions against our Lord. Christians of the past have seen signs they thought signified the end times. They even put a date on His second coming. But who are we, mere mortals, to try to determine God's timing. We should not question the Lord's timing. It will be as it always has been *perfect.*

Verse 19. There were even those who had been in their church body who departed deceived and, becoming antichrist, departed the faith. John says they were coming out from their midst because he says they were never of us could never accept either Jesus or the Father.

Verse 20. Our anointing comes from the holy one, our Lord and Savior Jesus Christ. That anointing and blessing is truly an undeserved gift but still a gift from our Lord. Remember to give Him thanks daily for that gift.

Verse 21. John continues to his readers the thought that they know the truth. If we know the truth, then we cannot lie. I refer to the previous thought: knowing that our words need to be true, our yes is yes, and no is no. Any lie is against His truth and brings shades of darkness into our personhood.

Verse 22. This powerful verse asks who the liar is. Is it one who denies that Jesus is the Christ, that He is the Son of God? John asks this question knowing very well who is the liar, and that is the spirit of antichrist. Their denial of Jesus being the Christ is one of Satan's ways of deceiving the people that they come in contact with. All that Satan says is a lie. His ways and lies attempt to influence both the new Christians and those who have been walking with the Lord for a long time.

Verse 23. If we deny Jesus because of Satan, then we do not have the Father in us; but if we confess that Jesus is the Son of God, then we have Jesus and also have the Father.

Verse 24. What have we heard from the beginning of the time when we came to know Jesus? How much is He within us? We heard the truth that Jesus is our Savior, and that must be in us. If He abides in us, then we will abide in the Son and in the Father.

Verse 25. Here is, again, a short but powerful verse. If the Lord makes a promise, it is going to be kept. The promise that He makes is *eternal life*. My question is, can we be Christlike? Can we (and do we) make our word good? I certainly hope so. I want my yes to be yes and my no to be no. It may seem simple, but the promise of *eternal life* is oh so powerful. What trust we can place in God's Word.

Verse 26. John tells us to be wary of deceivers. How can we best be wary? Reading His Word, studying the Word, ingesting the Word. Build up your strengths in Him by sharing His Word. Become a Bible scholar work both at it and into it. Don't play at it.

Reading this short verse, I am reminded of all the great writers of God's Word: Moses, the prophets, the gospels, Peter, Paul, and of others who contributed to these thoughts and ideas. As a writer, I always think about my past experiences, my present surroundings, and my future that is spending eternity with my Lord and Savior on the streets of heaven. I imagine hearing beautiful music of praise that has never been found on earth.

Verse 27. We have been given an anointing that is the Holy Spirit dwelling in each and every one of us. Fortunately, those who call upon Him are blessed with knowing Him. But it also doesn't mean that new Christians and even unbelievers can't experience the same gift. Come to Him. Ask Him to awaken in you. You must truly believe that He is present and is our helper. Jesus was not going to leave us alone; thus, the Holy Spirit was given to us as a gift from God. His son is a gift, as is the Holy Spirit, freely given. We must be willing to accept the gift that dwells within us.

Knowing that the Holy Spirit is present, I ask for the filling from head to toe. *Fill me, Lord.* Give me and teach me your ways through your spirit so that I may walk the righteous path you desire of me. The more direction and guidance the Holy Spirit imparts in us, the straighter our path becomes. Stay in His Word, *learn, pray,* and do His will in all we do.

Verse 28. As John asks of us and tells us to *abide* in Him, fall into Jesus; His arms await us. We must trust in the Lord that our sins have been forgiven by and through the blood of Jesus Christ. Yes, we have sinned and maybe we are holding on to past sins, thinking we are unworthy of being in His presence.

It does become a matter of faith—faith that says our sins are forgiven. Satan frequently attacks and lies to us, telling us how unworthy we are, and he wants us to believe his lies. But our Lord Jesus is coming to us, and His Holy Spirit is living in us. Thank you, Lord Jesus.

Verse 29. While comparing a couple of different Bible translations, I saw a change in the wording. One says to "do" righteous while the other says to "practice righteous living." This brings out the coach in me. I relate to the word *practice* quite well. I follow the philosophy that practice doesn't make perfect, but perfect practice makes perfect. I believe that our righteous walk is like a journey to perfection. We need to keep righteous thoughts in our minds so that the path we travel leads us to Christ.

The two verses 28 and 29 fit well together. When we fill our thoughts with Jesus and what He has done for us, we practice bringing Him into our minds. So that when problems occur (and they will), we will have perfectly practiced bringing Jesus into our lives. Our walk becomes stronger, more steady, and upright as we move along life's path.

Chapter 3

Verse 1. If John says we are called children of God, then we are His children. I do not doubt this. I do believe this is fantastic. To be brothers to all His children gives us a powerful force to move against the enemy. But in order for the world to recognize us as His children, the world must be made aware of our all-powerful God. So how can this be done? When people see a child that has similar characteristics to the parent, they say that the apple doesn't fall too far from the tree. Can we say the same? Do we love our Father so much that we walk the path of righteousness that He has set for us? Or do we become the rotten apple that no one picks up?

Our walk must be one that shines the light of Christ. How else will people know us as His children? Teach others by example or when asked, "Why are you so different?" you can tell them of the promise that is made to the children of God.

Verse 2. Confirmation of our inheritance comes when Jesus returns. His glory will show to all. We will then follow Him, being Christlike, as the Father will then instruct His children.

Verse 3. Do we have this hope? As we know we will see Him, we strive to purify ourselves, as He is pure. Our hope must stay focused on Him and not waver. Our hope yes, but until that day, we shall continue on the path that leads us to Jesus. Spread the good news that our Savior took our sins to the cross. But more importantly, His resurrection gives us the hope for eternal life with Him. To what standard does God hold us? In order to understand the standards, we must read and listen to the Word of God.

We must also be aware of the Holy Spirit tugging at our heart, making us aware of potential sin. The Holy Spirit is our guide, but do we shut Him down? Do we walk in righteousness daily? Each and every day, and sometimes each and every hour, we will pray for the Holy Spirit to awaken us in our life. Satan cannot stand against the Holy Trinity. He goes away. Do we feel that tug on our heart when we are heading in the opposite direction than the Lord wants us to go? It is the gift of our Counselor alerting us. *Pay attention!*

Keep God first in your life, remembering that we are not alone in this walk. We do not have to face adversity alone. Even when things go wrong, praise the Lord and stay faithful to Him.

Verse 4–5. Why was our Lord and Savior brought to earth? I see two reasons. The first is to redeem us, and the second is to show us the way that we should live. In the first, God's Son goes to the cross and bares the sins of the whole world. In the second, we are sinful in nature and fall short of God's glory in our walk. His perfection gives to us a model with His words, "Love your God with all your heart, mind, and soul," but also do likewise to your neighbor. *Romans 13:10* says, "Love worketh no ill to his neighbour: therefore love is the fulfilling of the law."

All are God's children. Should we, do we, love our brothers and sisters? Hopefully the answer is of course we do. Can we not see beyond the appearances, skin color, or status? We need to show Christlike love toward all of God's family. I know I keep returning to this thought, but that requires the indwelling of the Holy Spirit. That is what has been pressing on my heart and mind. Do we need that extra push to love those whom many see as one who is unlovable? The Holy Spirit can be that push. You can pray, "Holy Spirit, come. Give me the counsel and words to help me show God's love to individuals." I think that reading the body language of people gives clues to their feelings. Then even more important is discernment. Sometimes all that is needed is a smile with a friendly hello.

I'm so thankful for the wisdom the Holy Spirit provides. Jesus is the perfect one, we are not, but we are forgiven through claiming His shed blood.

Verse 6. Do we live the life that Christ wants us to live? If we do, then we do not live in sin. God wants us to follow the righteous path that Jesus sets for us. When we read and ingest the Word, we learn more and more of the way to stay on God's intended path. Jesus walked the earth to show us true love and servitude. Read of His mighty works and ways. Take them into your heart, soul, and mind. Is the potential to sin rampant in our society? Yes. We can see it, hear it, bump into it. It becomes difficult to avoid. Are we willing to not look, hear, or bump? If that is the case, then sin will have a difficult time planting its seed in us. I would much rather know our Savior than Satan. Study His Word. Work at it daily. Discipline yourself to build up your defenses against the sin that is in this world.

Verse 7. John could be calling them dear children because of his fatherly affection for those to whom he is writing. Or the child reference in this verse could refer to being young in Christ. We must be aware of the deceitful ways of Satan. As I said before, practice the discipline of coming closer to God. We do that through a strong prayer life, a regimen of quiet time in God's Word, and practicing His righteous ways. The more we practice, the stronger we become. I can't emphasize this thought enough. To know the Word isn't enough; we must put it into practice and follow Christ's example.

Lord, I thank you for your Son.

Verse 8. If our lack of discipline leads us to sin, then we are turning 180 degrees away from the righteous path and are heading toward the lies of Satan. It is mentioned that Satan (Lucifer, his former name) is a fallen angel that became the prince of darkness. His goal is to gather every soul that will believe his lies. Not only now but at the time of this book, sin is found in the world. God's timing of the appearance of His Son is always perfect. Jesus came to earth to teach, guide, and counsel us in His ways. His life shows us, by example, the type of life we should strive to live. But His death upon the cross broke the sins and the ways of Satan. His suffering, death, and resurrection bring us hope for eternal life with Him. He conquered the grave. He defeated Satan. He won the battle.

Verse 9. Are we born again? If you've answered yes, then we must not sin. That's a difficult assignment because we do sin, sometimes daily or even more frequently. We, who are born again, know and realize these two things: First, the Holy Spirit is God's gift to us, and the Holy Spirit lives within us. Second, when we ask God for forgiveness with a pure heart, then we trust that we are forgiven according to *1 John 1:9.* I frequently ask throughout the day for the Holy Spirit to give me needed guidance and counsel in my daily situations. I find myself speaking words that I know can only come from Him. When an activity becomes a blessing for another or myself, I know that God is present in all situations, and we give Him praise and thanksgiving.

Verse 10. It is a comforting thought to know that we are the children of God. Why? Because the Holy Spirit dwells in us, we can know this. Those who do not know that they are a child of God do not follow the righteous path. The passage reflects a selfish attitude of those who do not show love toward His brother or sister.

Selfishness and self-centeredness seems to be the accepted way of life today. Many individuals believe that it is their own work and abilities that got them to the top. They forget that God is the one who gifted them with those abilities. Sometimes they step on other people on their climb to the apex of their job. This, as we know, is totally unrighteous. Humbleness and gratitude are what is needed. Thanking the Lord for all that He has given to you, loving your brother as Christ has loved us.

Do not become swayed by unrighteous goals, but be swayed by the light of Jesus Christ. Come to God, and He will give you rest and comfort.

Verse 11. The thought of loving one another is crucial. We are all children of God. We can inherit what God has promised. Did someone do you wrong? Forgive him. Jesus, when asked, said to forgive seventy times seven. Don't keep count; just forgive. We all do wrong, and when one says to us, "I forgive you," we understand how that makes us feel. When we ask the Lord for forgiveness, we have the confidence that He will forgive us. Loving one another transcends all wrongs. Forgiveness of one's wrongs helps both the forgiven and the one who has been wronged. It is not a sign of weakness; it becomes a sign of righteousness. Love one another. Forgive their sin, remembering that Christ died on the cross to forgive our sins.

Verse 12. Cain's actions were being driven by the evil one, Satan, as he stirred up in Cain envy of God's favor that Abel had and he didn't. When I think of Cain's actions, I wonder how often the unrighteous thoughts of envy and unrighteousness get in the way. Abel's gifts were righteous, the ones that God wanted, while Cain's were not.

Through God's response, we can see the benefits, blessings, and gifts that come from following God's requests. Can those gifts provoke anger and envy in others who may want that? We must make those who think that way aware. That in order to receive those blessings, one must draw near to God. First, by our asking for the forgiveness our Lord and Savior, Jesus, died for. Then pray for God's guidance throughout the day so that Satan's lies will not affect us (lead us not into temptation). This thought continues on to the next verse.

Verse 13. The world may hate those they see as believers in Jesus Christ. Why be shocked by this? The world is surrounded by darkness, and when there are attempts to bring light into the world, those living in darkness try to extinguish it. As I stated before, the world is a dark place, and presently it seems to be getting darker. Evil forces are attempting to terrorize Christians at every turn. We must stay strong in our faith. Build our strength through prayer and His Word. Come to God when things seem to be turning darker. He is the light of the World. His promise is true. Listen to Him in your times of solitude, and the Holy Spirit will give you the guidance and direction that you seek.

Verse 14. This verse covers the fact that we love our brethren and can move from death to life eternal life. Do we truly show love for our brothers? It does help if we become aware of issues facing our brothers. I try to read the faces and body language of people. But some people do have the ability to mask their feelings. It might be due to shame of some sin or something else that they are trying to hide. I try not to pry if I suspect hidden things, but only try to show Christ's light around them. We must not show hatred toward others. It would be better yet to rid our heart of the hatred that may be present within us. We remember that we were created as children of God as others were also. I realize that softening our heart may be difficult toward someone who may have hurt us in some way, but we are the ones who must bring peace to our hearts and minds. How? Through God's help, we can bring forgiveness or understanding. Maybe even both. Holding on to hatred eats away at our heart and mind and is unrighteous and not healthy. John 1 represents the idea of love toward all.

Verse 15. Continuing on, the hatred toward a brother is equal to murder. We cannot have eternal life if hatred toward others is present within us. If what a brother has done is sinful, then we must pray for him. We don't have the power to forgive sin; only God can do that. But our hope for eternal life must be a softer heart toward a brother.

Verse 16. Do we truly recognize what Jesus did for us? He laid down His life for us. Why? Love is the answer, and as Christ our Savior has said in *John 15:13*, "Greater love hath no man than this, that a man lay down his life for his friends."

Few of us may be asked to follow this in a literal sense. But as the apostle Paul talked about dying daily in *1 Corinthians 15:31*, it refers to dying to our own desires, and I would say that would consists of many things which are a part of life. So what God has given to us that we are we willing to give up as a part of ourselves for a brother? Is it time in a hospital visit? A prison visit? Or are you using your talents to help someone? Our lives *do* get busy; but doing the *right* thing, the righteous thing, by sharing what God has blessed us with, is the giving up of a part of our life for them. I know many who give of themselves but not in a selfless or Godly manner. It's done in a self-serving way.

Bring Jesus into your life, and become the servant of men.

Verse 17. Do we have riches or wealth? Are we in love with money, or do we consider it God's blessing? It is all God's, and His blessing is meant to help those who are in need. I was told many years ago that if everyone tithed, we would not have any need for government help. But the churches would need to be filled, and the government would have to step out of the way and allow God's blessings to flow.

Express your love to those in need. This is the righteous and godly thing to do.

Verse 18. It is easy to say what people want to hear. Lip service is frequent in our society. Now, I do believe in being positive and encouraging in my words. But more important than what we say, we must back up our words with positive actions. Be truthful in what is said *and done.* True actions reflect righteousness. Don't just say to your spouse or boss, "I'll get right to that," hoping that will eliminate the present issue. It is better to say in a truthful way, "I am presently busy working on this or that, and I will get to it as soon as I get this done." That may add some stress to your day, but you are being truthful.

Another way to back up your words is saying to yourself that your yes *is* yes, and your no *is* no.

Be truthful and righteous in your deeds and words. This, in turn, will make your life more godly and a whole lot easier.

Verse 19. When we practice truthfulness, our heart is at ease. When we are truthful, we are assured that we are doing God's will. God is truth, and if we say we are of God, then the truth must reside in our hearts. We must trust this and remove all deceit and lies from our heart.

Reside, Holy Spirit, in us. Continue to purify our heart, soul, and mind.

Verse 20. Sometimes, when we look in the mirror, we are not happy with who we see looking back at us. Do we attempt to mask our wrongs? Or do we beat ourselves up for our sins? God is a greater mirror. He knows our heart. But regardless of what we see or think of ourselves, we must remember the unfailing love of our Lord and Savior.

When Satan attacks, and he will attempt to bring us down to his level, we must return to God. Satan does not want to hear the name of Jesus coming from our mouths or our thoughts. He flees at His name. God loves us. He hears us and feels our shortcomings.

Thank you, Lord, for your unending, never failing love.

Verse 21. If God is in our hearts, then why should we be so harsh upon ourselves? Our trust in the fact that God resides in us is so wonderful. His love and mercy surrounds us. Today, people like to think of living in a bubble, and heaven forbid if anyone should try to enter that bubble. My choice is that the bubble that surrounds me is the Holy Spirit. Let that light shine through the bubble so that all will see is the light of Jesus shining through me.

Have we all sinned? Yes we have. But our forgiveness and redemption has been bought and paid for by our Lord and Savior, Jesus Christ.

Verse 22. Do we go to God in prayer with a pure heart? If not, we need to ask for the hardening of our heart to be broken and remade. Do we still hold on to anger toward a brother? Ask the Lord to lead us to forgive and let go of that anger and hurt. We want and need to lead a godly life. Trust the Lord for guidance to keep His commandments. Please the Lord in all that we do. As we look at and study Jesus's life upon the earth, we find He was the greatest servant of man. From taking care of the poor to His death on the cross, *He gave*!

Can we do what is pleasing to God? Ask Him daily for guidance to do His will. Keep Him in your heart. Trust Him to lead you upon the path of righteousness.

Verse 23. A simple but powerful verse. His commandment is to believe in His name and to love one another. That is the path that we need to follow. Jesus is the light leading us, and His love pours out from us to our brothers. He will show us the need; we then need to take the action. Trust in the Lord that He will give us the strength and wisdom to do His will.

Verse 24. The conditions are set. To abide in Christ is to follow His commandments, and then we know He abides in us. Sometimes we become blind and deaf to His guidance. It becomes a matter of faith and trust. But the Holy Spirit in us assures us of Christ's presence within.

Call upon Him daily for guidance. God is in us, wanting us to rely on Him for all that we do. Come in prayer, oh faithful one, and He will lead and guide us.

Chapter 4

Within this fourth chapter of 1 John, there is found a powerful message of love. In the 21 verses, the word *love* is found twenty-five times, and this does not count the term *beloved*. We know the word *love* is powerful. It goes beyond fondness, like, or infatuation. In dictionary definition, we find many meanings of love. Among those that are found in the Bible are "God's benevolence and mercy toward man" or "man's devotion or adoration of God." Also the benevolence, kindness, or brotherhood that man should rightfully feel toward others. That word *love*, when said between two people, must be said with meaning rather than out of habit. And of course, God's love is most powerful.

Verse 1. This verse warns us to be wary of those who speak false words. Our awareness stems from knowing and understanding God's Word. If something doesn't seem in line with God, it probably isn't. There were false prophets in John's time as there are today. I think these individuals look at the effect that our Lord has and try to match it to their own agenda. No one on earth can match Jesus. All we can do is deliver His Word and allow God to do the rest.

Be aware of those who switch doctrine to their own. We need to stick to His Word. Study constantly and learn.

Verse 2. Do we daily confess that Jesus Christ is Lord? Those who do not confess Jesus to be the Son of God are false spirits. I think of the so-called theologians who admit that Jesus walked the earth but refuse to recognize Him as the Son of God.

Jesus came to earth from God. No one has ever had the influence upon man that Jesus had. How else could that influence be anything else except from God? This is our foundation. That Jesus is Lord, and then everything else falls away.

Verse 3. In John's times, they recognized the presence of the spirit of antichrist. Satan is powerful, and as we all know, he just doesn't give up. He wants our souls, and his lies and deceit are constantly surrounding us. Prepare and strengthen yourselves for those attacks. Put on the full armor, as Paul refers to in Ephesians 6:10, to fend off Satan and his desires for us.

Verse 4. Satan is in the world. His darkness is like a cloud covering the sun. Remember, children, you have overcome those attacks; and even though they are always present, the Holy Spirit is also always present. Call on Him when you feel the attacks coming. He is greater than any attack against you. Satan does not want to take on the Holy Spirit. Therefore, you must keep the Holy Spirit alive in you. He gives you the needed guidance and protection. Remember that the Lord has given you free will, and that free will also allow the Holy Spirit to be your guide.

Verse 5–6. These two verses regard our freedoms of choice. (5) That those in the world speak from the world's perspective. We have the choice to either listen or to (6) know we are from God and choose to listen to those who speak of God. The rest of the world may not listen to the Word of God, but we know the truth. The spirit of truth is in us. If it's not, then that becomes the spirit of error.

Verse 7–12. These verses are well-known as the brotherly love verses. The word *love* is found twelve times in these verses. We are told to love one another as love is from God, and all that is from God is good *(Mark 10:18)*. At Christmastime, we remember God's great love. He sent His Son so that we would learn to live through Him. When I reflect on these words, they are not seasonal; they are permanently etched on our minds.

God's love surrounds us. I know we say in both word and song that we wish these feelings would last all year. Guess what! They can when we start each day with giving thanks to the Lord for His great love. His Son, who, some thirty-three years after appearing on earth, went to the cross and took away our sins by washing them away with His blood. Such great love.

So as we see the story of His love, His gift, let us remember it by starting each new day thanking the Lord for his gift of *love*.

Verse 13. God's gift of the Holy Spirit gives us confidence that God dwells in us. Not only does He live within us, but we also live in Him. The *confidence* that we have in Him is the basis for the faith that we have in Him. John frequently refers to the times that he has spent with Jesus but we haven't, so we have faith that God dwells in us.

Verse 14. We know from the testimonies of John and his con-temporaries, which are recorded in the Word of God, that Jesus was sent to the world as its Savior.

Verse 15. We know from the Word that Jesus was sent. Why would we have any doubts? His death upon the cross took our sins away. His resurrection gives us the hope of eternal life in paradise with Him. When we confess that Jesus is the Son of God, Jesus lives in us. We also abide in God. What a place to spend eternity.

Verse 16. This verse stresses God's love for us, and that He is love. We need to live in love toward all. Do we? Do we want God living in us? Practice love—true love—toward all.

Verse 17. On judgment day, can we come before the Lord with love in our hearts? We need to and should want to live a life full of God's love toward our brothers. Can we cast aside hate, jealousy, or any other unrighteous thoughts or actions toward our brothers? If we can't, pray for a pure heart, one filled with true love toward our brothers, for we are to display Jesus in this world.

Verse 18. Love is pure and fearless. As we develop purer hearts full of love, we become more Christlike. Do we have any doubts and fears that our hearts and love must be perfected? Are we perfect? *No way!* But this is something for which we are striving.

Verse 19. When we doubt *our* love, *we must* remember what Christ did for us. He first loved us. I often think how amazing His love for us is. How we, as sinners, are forgiven and confess that Jesus is Lord. Our complex society seems so rushed that it is difficult to slow down and return to God. We are inundated with so many things that try to pull us away from God and forget how we should start each day.

Build up your strength, remembering that He first loved us.

Verse 20–21. Love the Lord our God, but also love your brother. Anything else is ungodly. Hatred, deceit, and hidden agendas pull us away from the righteous path. Love your brother, and do things out of pure love. Jesus is pure love. His Word is all about love! Our God's love for us.

Chapter 5

Verse 1. Do we believe that Jesus is the Son of God? If we do, then we love both the Son and the Father. I am amazed at the emphasis placed on the word *love* and the number of times we are reminded to love both the Son, Jesus, and God who sent Him to us.

Verse 2. As was previously stated, we must love our brothers, who are also children of God. When we love them, we love God. Keep His commandments, but first we must love God.

Verse 3. God loves us to keep His commandments. How? By loving God. The commandments are for our own good. By keeping them, we exhibit God's love. First, we show God's love is within us. Second, we pour out His love toward others. Are others seeing you as different in this world? If God is living in you, then others should see that. Pour out His love. Live by His commandments. Love the children of God.

Verse 4. We are overcomers. We have faith. We know that what the world throws at us is not strong enough to pull us away from God.

Verse 5. Do you believe that Jesus is the Son of God? With an answer of yes to the question, we know that we can overcome any adversity. That is the issue. We know the life of Jesus here on earth, His walk, His death, His resurrection. All these give us hope for life eternal with Him.

Verse 6. Christ was given to us as a gift from God. He was baptized with water and died on the cross, shedding His blood for our sins. From the time of His temptation by Satan until the cross, His life shows us one thing: *love.* All of Satan's temptations could not pull Him away from the love of God. Then His final act of love, the shedding of His blood, taking away our sins. What great *love.*

Verse 7–8. The expression of the Trinity is powerful. Can I get beyond the complexity of the Trinity? I hope so. God is Three in One, enough said! The Father in heaven, God, affirms our relationship. When the Word walked upon the earth and since He ascended, He makes intercession for us. And the Holy Spirit was sent to intercede as our advocate on earth on our behalf. On earth, the Spirit descended on Jesus in the waters of baptism. On the cross, Jesus's blood bought our eternal life. Today, the Spirit works through the church on earth. The waters of baptism tell others that we are born of God because His blood was shed for us. Such a great gift. What great gifts of God, His Son and the Holy Spirit.

Holy Spirit of God, almighty indwelling within us, be our counselor, our protector, and our healer.

Verse 9. As much as we hear the witness of men, always remember that the Word comes to us through His Son.

Verse 10–11. We build ourselves up to be a strong witness for God with our belief that Jesus is the Son of God. If we do not believe this, then we make God a liar. God can't and does not lie. Why should we not believe that Jesus is His Son? If that is our thought, then we don't believe in God.

John's thoughts have been leading to this verse. God gives us eternal life through His Son, Jesus Christ. Love, faith, and belief in God's Word are found in this verse. Jesus's life upon the earth gives us access to eternal life, faith, hope, and love. I return to Paul's letter to the Corinthians, "The greatest of these is love" *(1 Cor. 13:13, New International Version [NIV]).* All that we do must be done in love, and the same thought of love must occupy our thoughts. Understand God's love for us.

Verse 12. Simply stated, do we have Jesus in our hearts? If so, then we have eternal life. If not, then we are missing the train to eternal life in heaven.

Verse 13. For you who believe in the name of Jesus as the Son of God, this is my purpose in writing these things. John is emphasizing the point that if you want to have eternal life, you must believe in the name of Jesus as the Son of God. If you do, you *know* you have eternal life.

Verse 14. When we pray, do we have assurance that if asked in accordance to His will, will our prayer be heard? Remember that God answers prayer, but in a threefold manner. *Yes, no* and *wait*!

Verse 15. We have the faith that God hears our prayers. If done with a pure heart and in line with God's will for us, then our prayers will be heard and answered.

Verse 16. Do we see sin in others? Pray for them. It is not enough to pray for ourself and family. If we are aware of others committing sin, we need to also pray for them. I believe in prayer for the unsaved and for those who are falling away from God. Seeing troubled brothers and sisters should lead us to pray for them, in public or in private. All sin can be pardoned, but some may have moved into a state where they are no longer convicted by the Holy Spirit because of callousness. Our prayers may help bring some peace to them. Allow God to handle their situation.

Verse 17. Sin is anything that is not right in God's eyes, but none of it leads to death if confessed and forgiven. Prayer brings hope.

Verse 18. Some confusion may come from this verse. It says that if we are born of God, then we don't want to sin. If we are born of God, we do not serve sin. This means that we do not want to continue on with that sin. We must ask for forgiveness, lay it down at the cross and which then will prevent Satan from have control over or harming our lives.

Verse 19. The entire world is wrapped up in wickedness and sin. We, however, are not of this world but of God. Temptations are all around, and we cannot crawl up the mountain and hide away. We are called to spread the good news in a dark world. Be the light, spread the word, and allow God to work His miracles.

Verse 20. We know the truth. We know Jesus is truth. The promise of coming to Jesus is the promise of eternal life.

Verse 21. One last warning is given to stay away from idols. Have no other god but God who is eternal and the life-giving God. Idols and superficial loves exist in our world today from technology to false prophets. Keep away from those things that you may worship more than God. Strengthen yourself daily, pray, fellowship with other believers for strength, grow in your faith that Jesus is the Son of God, as is *love*.

2 John

This letter is one of encouragement, reminder, and warning to keep the faith and holding on to truth. The main points of emphasis are walking in our Savior's commandments and that our Savior is both truth and love.

Verse 1. This letter is addressed to the elect lady and her children. This is thought to be a reference to the church itself and its members. Others think it may be referring to a more notable lady who has come into the church, such as a dignitary. I don't think this is correct due to the equality of all believers, no matter their station in life. John recognizes the reputation of the church and faith of her members. John complements their walk in righteousness.

Verse 2. The word *truth* is mentioned three times in the first two verses and four times in the first three verses. Thus, there is emphasis upon the word *truth*. Truth, by definition, is consistency of statements to correlate with the facts of reality. To make it even simpler, the facts themselves.

God's truth dwells within us forever. Jesus is truth. His words are truth. God's words are infallible. He cannot lie.

Verse 3. When we have truth within us, we also obtain grace, mercy, and peace.

Verse 4. John mentions her children as walking in truth in the same way that we desire our children to do. Why do we walk in truth? It is because we have received His commandments. *That* is the truth, the way, and the life.

Verse 5. From the beginning, John reminds her of the commandment to love one another. When you think about it, *love one another* is such a simple statement and easy to do when things are flowing smoothly. But do we keep that thought in mind when persecution, false statements, hurtful words are sent our way?

Verse 6. We have here an answer to the last question. We show our love for Christ as we obey all the commandments. We show our love as we obey that commandment no matter what. Continue to walk in obedience.

Verse 7. This verse brings to mind the deceivers, those antichrist, and those who do not believe in Jesus. We should always be on guard against these forces. Satan is always working to place doubts in our minds regarding Jesus being the Son of God.

Verse 8. Be *diligent*! Hold close to you those things God has already accomplished in you. Cast away the thoughts from Satan. Remember always the reward that we have.

Verse 9. Because sin destroys our relationship with God, build up strength in the Lord, read His Word, listen to and follow godly people. This will lead to a stronger relationship with the Lord and His Son.

Verse 10. Do not associate with those who profess false teachings. Do not allow them into your house. In our world today, there are many ways that these false teachings can come into our houses. It doesn't have to be done by a person in particular, but our mass communications tools can and do bring in these false teachings.

Verse 11. If we open up that door (TV, music, the computer), we then take part in the evil of Satan. He says just take a glimpse of this or listen to this one song. These things have the ability to attract us and pull us back into the world. Satan is not truthful, lie upon lie, deceit upon deceit. He is enticing us to fall into his trap. If we partake in these things, we are working hand in hand with him.

Verse 12. In conclusion, John wishes to talk face-to-face. In our world today, with all the methods of communication available face-to-face is becoming passé. I wonder about a couple of things. One, are all the words transmitted understood totally by the receiver? Two, in what direction is our world heading when individual conversations are being thrown overboard?

Being present with the one you wish to speak to is a lot more pleasurable than in any other form of communication.

Verse 13. I want pass along the greetings of the children of the elect lady here which would refer to the local church where he was and its membership.

3 John

Gaius was the one to whom this third epistle was written. He was beloved by John due to his actions in dealing with travelers, giving aid and comfort to those carrying the message of Jesus Christ.

Verse 1. John's greetings to Gaius is one of respect and love. We need to do the same when meeting a respected elder.

Verse 2. Not only does John pray for his physical well-being but also his spiritual health.

Do we lack for words in prayer? Why not pray for the leaders in the church that they will be well in mind, body, and spirit.

Verse 3–4. How well do we receive good messages about people? Or does jealousy or other thoughts creep in?

John shows true joy regarding Gaius and his work. We need to be happy for those who experience joy also.

Verse 5. Be an encourager to those who are doing Christ's work. If we see someone who is doing God's work but may be struggling, say or write something encouraging. Lift that person up to help them in doing God's work.

Verse 6. It does not behoove us to brag about our own doings and actions. It is much better that those who you helped bring forth your good works. Don't be prideful, and send messages out about your good works.

Verse 7–8. Those traveling and spreading the good news should not receive anything from nonbelievers. It becomes the responsibility of the believers to help shelter, feed, and give financial support if needed.

Verse 9–11. Followers of Jesus should not be trying to hold domination over all others. If someone within the church is found to be sending out false messages, this issue needs to be addressed. Do not become followers of those whose words are not from God.

Verse 12. Again make mention to others of the good work that is being done by others. This will encourage them by the words of others.

Verse 13–14. As in 2 John, John wishes to continue his message, not in writing though but face-to-face conversation.

II

Maureen Ritari

9

Soldier or Warrior?

Are you a soldier or warrior for Christ? Are you thinking, *Well, aren't they the same?* No, they are not. All warriors are soldiers, but not all soldiers are warriors. The dictionary's definitions for soldiers are as follows:

- A person who works for a specified cause
- (Ant/termite) serving as a fighter in defense of the colony
- Low-ranking member in a crime organization
- One who shirks their duty, pretends to work, a loafer

When I think of soldiers in the Bible, I picture the Roman soldiers. I think because they made their presence known. They were working for a specific cause to increase the Roman Empire and to keep everyone in check. They were also low-level ranking men (like the crime organization) just doing what they were told to do. Even those that arrested and crucified Jesus were doing what they were told to do.

In the Old Testament, men were fighting in defense of their colony (country), protecting their people. These are military reasons. But how should or would we look if we are soldiers for Christ? If we are told by God to do something, will we obey? Or are we going to work for His cause and defend His Word, truth, and church? Maybe we will be like the fourth definition, where we are shirking our responsibility, pretending we are living for Christ but really aren't, saying the right things but not living it, being so consumed with our everyday life that we forget that our Lord has called us to be His soldiers.

So what's the difference between a soldier and a warrior? The first scripture I found for warrior was *Exodus 15:3 (NIV)*, "The Lord is a warrior, The Lord is His name." The message paraphrase includes the words "your strong right hand shatters the enemy."

Our Lord is a warrior. So what is the dictionary definition of a warrior?

- A person engaged or experienced in warfare
- A person engaged in some struggle or conflict, fighting man
- A person who shows or has shown great vigor, courage, or aggressiveness

I looked back in the Bible for other verses about warriors. The first person after the Lord that I found called a warrior was Gideon.

> The Angel of the Lord appeared to him and told him, "The Lord is with you, you valiant warrior!" (*Judg. 6:12–13, NASB*)

But in *verse 13*, Gideon questions the Lord about abandoning His people.

In *Judges 6:14*, it states,

> The Lord looked at him and said "Go in this your strength and deliver Israel from the land of Midian. Have I not sent you?"

In *verse 15* again, Gideon is questioning the Lord about how he can deliver Israel. He is basically saying, "My family is nothing, and I am the youngest of the nothing."

Verse 16 says,

> The Lord said "Surely, I will be with you and you shall defeat Midian as one man."

God called him a valiant warrior, but Gideon kept asking God for assurance that He would be with him. Where is his faith and trust in God? If God is a warrior and He is in us, then shouldn't we be warriors too? But aren't we like Gideon sometimes? God tells us to do something and we think, *Why are you telling me? I am nothing.* He tells us, "I will be there," but we keep asking, "Are you sure it is supposed to be me?" When He sends us, He will equip us.

The next warrior was David. As a youth, he slew Goliath *(1 Sam. 17:37)*. David isn't called a warrior, but he has God's strength, and he fits the definition of a warrior, a person engaged in some struggle, conflict (lions, bears), and showing great vigor, courage, and aggressiveness. Vigor means active strength or force, healthy mental or physical energy or power. Doesn't that sound like David?

Courage is the quality of mind or spirit that enables a person to face difficulty, danger, and pain without fear. David, as a youth, had the courage to face a giant. He sounds like a warrior to me.

In *1 Chronicles 12:1–22*, David is hiding from Saul, and men come to his defense. He says a warrior needs to sling stones and shoot arrow from a bow (trained in warfare). When he was in the stronghold in the wilderness, he said a warrior is a mighty man of valor, trained for war, could handle shield and spear, have faces like the faces of a lion, and swift as a gazelle. I believe these men started as soldiers, but as they continued to get closer to David, spending time in his presence, they evolved into warriors like their commander. *First Chronicles 12:22* says, "Day by day men came to help David until there was a great army, like the army of God."

So before I told you all warriors are soldiers, but all soldiers aren't warriors. So how do you become a soldier? First, I guess you have to ask yourself, do you want to be a soldier for Christ, and if so, what kind? Are you going to work for a specific cause (God's truth), defend your colony (Christ, church, family), or be a loafer and pretend you're working when you really aren't.

In *2 Timothy 2:3–4*, Paul says, "Suffer hardships with me, as a good soldier of Christ Jesus. No soldier in active service entangles himself in the affairs of everyday life; so that he may please the one who enlisted him as a soldier."

So what are hardships? Hardships are leaving behind worldly security and rigorous discipline, be willing to sacrifice and suffer to achieve a goal. If you think about our servicemen, they suffer these hardships. They leave cozy houses, family, and safety. In their training, there is rigorous discipline, as well as sacrificing their lives to protect our country and others, which is their goal.

Paul is trying to enlist soldiers to help him win people to Christ. He is letting them know that there are sacrifices a soldier has to make, but they do it for the thought of victory. As a soldier for Christ, we will have hardships, struggles, and have to be disciplined in the things of Christ. However, our victory is eternal life with Him. We have to stay faithful, trust in the Lord, and rely on His strength so we will be victorious.

My question to you now is: Do you want to remain a soldier, or do you want to be a warrior? Our Lord is a warrior. *Exodus 15:3* says so. If the Lord is in us, shouldn't we be a warrior and not settle for being a soldier? How do we become a warrior? *First Chronicles 12* says we become men and women who sling stones and shoot arrows. What does that mean? It means we use scripture to fight the enemy. In *1 Chronicles 12:8*, it says we are to become men and women of valor. That means to have heroic courage, bravery, and boldness or determination in the face of great danger.

Draw on God's strength. We are also to be trained for war. To do this, we need to spend time in God's Word, in prayer, and in His presence, trusting and having faith in the Lord. We are also to hold a shield and a spear. To me, that is putting on the full armor of God.

Put on the full armor of God, so that you will be able to stand firm against the schemes of the devil. For our struggle is not against flesh and blood, but against the rulers, against the powers, against the world forces of this darkness, against the spiritual forces of wickedness in the heavenly places. Therefore, take up the full armor of God, so that you will be able to resist in the evil day, and having done everything, to stand firm. *(Eph. 6:11–13)*

So let's go back and look at the definition of a warrior:

- A person engaged and experienced in warfare (conflict, struggle between two enemies).

     The devil is our enemy. So everything he has thrown at us has given us the experience to fight. As mothers, we fight for our kids. Don't mess with the mother bear!
- A person engaged in some struggle or conflict.

     All of us have had struggles and issues—family, health, finances, jobs, etc.
- A person who has shown or shows great vigor, courage or aggressiveness.

To me, this isn't getting in people's faces, being loud, or fighting; it's just standing up for God's truth in any circumstance, standing strong in Holy Spirit power. In today's society, this is what we need. We need to show courage and be true to our faith in the Lord.

I believe that God wants us all to be warriors and warrior princesses. I say warrior princess because when I was in prayer, He kept saying warrior princess. This led me to this message. I am also believing that He said it because that's what I am, a warrior princess.

If we all become warriors, we will be like the men who came to David. As we warriors continue to come to Christ, there will be an army like the army of God. So I leave you with this: Are you going to be a soldier or a warrior for Christ?

10

Do You *Know* Jesus or Just Know of Him?

Do you know Jesus or just know of Him? There are many in the world who will say they believe in Jesus, but what does that mean?

- Do you believe He is the Son of God?
- Do you believe He was a prophet, carpenter, or just a man?
- Do you believe He is the light of the world, Lord, and Savior?

"I believe" can mean a lot of things. But is it believing that He exists, knowing Jesus, or simply knowing of Him? In my opinion, for many, it is just knowing of Him. So when or how does it change to knowing Him?

Well, how do we get to know someone? We usually strike up a conversation where we start to learn about them, their likes, dislikes, interests, etc. We also will spend time together, sharing experiences. As we grow closer and begin to trust them, we start to share the hurts, frustrations, and trials we go through, as well as the good things (promotions, births, etc.).

That is also the way we get to know our Lord. We talk to Him, spend time with Him, read His Word, and experience His presence. The more we do these things, the closer we get and the better we know Him. As hurts, trials, and frustrations come our way, He is the one we turn to. He should also be the first one we go to for the good things as well because they are blessings from Him. If we don't take the time to get to know Him, we will only know *of* Him. We will be like the large percentage of the world.

I remember when I went from knowing *of* Him to the beginning of my journey to knowing Him. When we know Him, we have a relationship with Him. He's just like a friend. We all have different friendships; they are either casual or close. Casual friendships are people who you might talk to occasionally, but you typically wouldn't spend a lot of time with, except maybe in a social setting. There is not a strong emotional bond.

Close friendships have a strong emotional bond, and they develop over time. They are the ones you will trust with your deepest thoughts and fears. You know they will always be there for you, supporting you and being that shoulder to lean on. Close friends will also tell us when we are wrong without the fear of losing our friendship.

Close friendships don't just happen overnight. It's a process that takes time and energy. They don't just happen. You have to make the effort to stay in contact and communicate with them. If we don't, what happens? We start to drift apart. Ask yourself, is Jesus a close or casual friend?

As I have grown in my relationship with the Lord, I consider Him to be a close friend. I experience His love, forgiveness, peace, and blessings. But can I learn more? Of course. God is omniscient.

We will never fully know and understand Him in our lifetime. However, that doesn't mean we stop trying. When we stop trying, we begin to drift away, and we relegate Him to the casual friend category instead of the close friend category.

Let's not be like those in the world who know of Him. Let's ask Him to be our closest friend and truly know Him.

11

Patience and Waiting on God's Timing

Patience definition:

1. Quality of being patient, as bearing of provocation, annoyance, misfortune, or pain without complaint, loss of temper, irritation or the like
2. An ability or willingness to suppress restlessness or annoyance when confronted with delay
3. Quiet, steady perseverance; even tempered care, diligence, endurance

Patience and God's timing is written throughout the Bible. Unfortunately, we (just like some in the Bible) have a tendency to be impatient, and because of that, we start to take things into our own hands instead of waiting for God's timing. We forget that God has perfect timing and reasons for why He waits. He knows the plan He has for us. We just don't. "'For I know the plans I have for you,' declares the LORD, 'plans to prosper you and not to harm you, plans to give you hope and a future'" *(Jer. 29:11, NIV)*.

As I look back throughout my life in retrospect, I now see His perfect timing. I know there are women that have tried to have a child. We get this whole plan in our head that we have everything timed out just right. I will have my first child, then two years, later the second, and so on. But I found out that my plans weren't God's plan. I wanted my children about two years apart so they could go to high school together. I had no problem getting pregnant with my first daughter (Shannon). So I figured it would happen again right away. Well, it didn't. I couldn't figure why. We tried for about a year and a half. Finally, I was pregnant again. Things were going smoothly until Holy Thursday of April 1990. I was driving to work and slid on black ice going over a bridge on I-90. I was 7seven months pregnant. My 4Runner flipped end over end in a ditch, and I ended upside down. I was able to get out of the truck. I didn't have a scratch on me, my baby was fine, but my truck was crushed everywhere except the driver's side. I believe God was watching over us!

That night, I just fell on my bed and cried. "Lord, why am I here? My baby and I should be dead, but you saved us." I believed in God and thought I had faith, but that day, a true relationship began. I grew closer to God and started reading His Word daily.

You see, I realized a few months later that was all in His plan and perfect timing. I was due with my second daughter (Kelsey) on June 9, 1990, which was also my mom and dad's wedding anniversary. At this time, they were living out of state. On that night I called them, not to tell them they had a new granddaughter, but that their youngest son had been in a motorcycle accident. He was life-flighted to Erie. At that time, we knew he had hit his head, but he was responding. So they decided to get up early and head this way. By the time they arrived, he was no longer responding. His brain stem swelled, and within the next few hours, he was considered brain dead. Kelsey was born two days after his funeral.

As I looked back at this time, I saw God's hand in it all. I wanted my kids two and a half years apart, but God's timing was for Kelsey to be born at that perfect time. At a time of sorrow, she brought joy. She kept us occupied so we didn't dwell on the loss of my brother. My accident was also God's perfect timing. Because I developed a relationship with Him, I was able to trust Him with my grief. I was able to deal with my loss by going to God. If that had not happened, I am not sure how I would have handled my grief. There are things we all have going on in our life now that we have to be patient and trust in God's timing.

One of the people in the Old Testament that waited for God's perfect timing was Noah. *Genesis 8:6–16* says, "Noah patiently waited for the waters to recede." He waited for God's time. In *John 11:5–7*, Lazarus was raised from the dead. Why did Jesus wait? If Jesus would have just healed Lazarus before he died, then the people could have said he really wasn't sick. But you couldn't deny that someone was dead, buried, and then alive. There were many witnesses. He delayed for a purpose. It was to be on His timing. He knew He was going to heal Lazarus.

When God doesn't answer in our time, we think He isn't listening or answering our prayer. The way we want things answered aren't always God's answer. He will meet our needs according to His perfect time. We have to wait patiently.

The Old and New Testaments talk about patience (or lack of it) and God's patience toward us. In *Genesis 29*, Jacob was very patient. He worked fourteen years for Rachel because Laban deceived him. He wanted Rachel for his wife. It was important to him, so waiting and working fourteen years for her was worth it.

In *Genesis 30*, Rachel had been wanting a child. Her sister was giving Jacob children, but she wasn't. God remembered her and opened her womb, but not before she had taken things into her own hands. She had become impatient. Because of her impatience, there were consequences to her actions. There was strife and jealousy among the children.

How many of us have been like Rachel? Being impatient and taking things into our own hands. It is hard to wait on the Lord, but we are to trust in Him and have patience and courage while we wait. It is better than living with the consequences that occur when we try to do things ourselves. Patience is hardest when we need it the most. But it is the key to achieving our goals and desires.

Sometimes God uses delays to test our patience. In *1 Samuel 13:11–12*, Saul took things into his own hands because he didn't have the patience to wait for Samuel. He offered the burned offering which was strictly forbidden. Saul knew he wasn't supposed to offer the burned offering. He said that Samuel, by delaying his arrival, forced him. Nobody was twisting his arm. He was losing control of the people and took things into his own hands instead of waiting for Samuel. Sometimes God delays because he wants to see how we will react. Because Saul's pride was being challenged, he wouldn't wait. So he was going to have to suffer the consequences: the loss of his kingdom.

How many of us start to take things into our own hands instead of waiting on the Lord. We choose to do things we shouldn't. Maybe it's a decision about a job, relationship, house, car, etc. We have prayed and we don't have an answer when we want it, so we just forge ahead with our own way. These might be times God is testing us to see if we are going to be patient and wait on His timing. But when things don't work out, we blame God instead of looking at ourselves. We didn't wait, so we have to face the consequences and hopefully learn from our mistake.

Second Samuel 5:4–5 says, "David was thirty years old when he became king, and he reigned forty years. At Hebron he reigned over Judah seven years and six months, and in Jerusalem he reigned thirty-three years over all Israel and Judah."

David reigned for forty years. His patience was also tested. David was young when Samuel anointed him, a teenager, but he didn't become king until he was thirty. That was probably around fifteen years after he was anointed. Throughout those years, there were times he could have taken things into his own hands to become king. He didn't. David had opportunities to kill Saul and become king. Instead, he patiently waited on the Lord's timing. He continued to live his life, gaining in strength and wisdom by spending time in the presence of his King.

If David would have taken Saul's life into his own hands, his reign would not have been blessed. When we take things into our own hands that are not God's plan, then they are not blessed. When we repent and trust in Him, He can take our messes and bring good out of them.

Look what happened with David and Bathsheba when he took her. Not only did he sin in taking her, but he also had her husband killed. The consequence to this was the loss of their son. However, he repented, and God continued to bless him, though he had a lot of heartache following his sin.

There are times we might have to wait years for answers, fulfilled promises, or healings. If we wait, the blessings will be abundant in comparison to what would happen when we take matters into our own hands.

God is patient toward us. It says in *Genesis 19:24*, "Then the Lord rained on Sodom and Gomorrah brimstone and fire from the Lord out of heaven." God was patient with sparing the wicked cities for ten good people. But then He had enough.

As we grow, we develop a deeper love for God because we have a better understanding of His patience with us when we continually sin. In *Nehemiah 9:16–21*, Israel was stubborn and did not follow God's commandments. God was still with them in the wilderness. He guided them night and day. He provided for them for forty years even when they complained and made a calf of molten medal.

Even though God is patient with us, we can't mistake His patience for approval. He is just waiting for us to change. He is giving us time to repent, look at ourselves, and see what needs to change. We should all be in awe of God's patience because we all deserve His judgment *(Rom. 2:4)*.

> For if you ever go back and cling to the rest of these nations, these which remain among you, and intermarry with them, so that you associate with them and they with you, know with certainty that the LORD your God will not continue to drive these nations out from before you; but they will be a snare and a trap to you, and a whip on your sides and thorns in your eyes, until you perish from off this good land which the LORD your God has given you. Now behold, today I am going the way of all the earth, and you know in all your hearts and in all your souls that not one word of all the good words which the LORD your God spoke concerning you has failed; all have

been fulfilled for you, not one of them has failed.
It shall come about that just as all the good words
which the LORD your God spoke to you have
come upon you, so the LORD will bring upon you
all the threats, until He has destroyed you from
off this good land which the LORD your God has
given you. When you transgress the covenant
of the LORD your God, which He commanded
you, and go and serve other gods and bow down
to them, then the anger of the LORD will burn
against you, and you will perish quickly from off
the good land which He has given you. *(Josh. 23:
12–16, NASB)*

The Israelites were told not to intermarry. If they did, it would
be a snare and a trap to them. God was faithful and fulfilled His
words and promises to them, but they still turned away and trans-
gressed against the covenant of God. God will be patient for only so
long. If we continue to serve other gods (like Israel), He will eventually bring His righteous judgment.

In *Isaiah 6:9–13*, Judah continually exhausted God's patience.
They wouldn't listen until cities were destroyed and they had nowhere
to go for help. They were at the bottom of the barrel, so to speak. He
wants us to go to Him. But He wants to be first, not last. Do we wait
to go to Him as a last resort? We don't listen to Him, so we screw
things up. We should be listening to Him first. Unfortunately, we
like to do our own thing and think God will always be there to get
us out of the mess He told us not to do in the first place. We need to
listen now before we try Him so much that His patience runs out.

God's patience will eventually turn to anger. In *Psalm 74:1–2*,
God's patience with Israel had worn out. He got tired of waiting for
them to stop sinning and repent; to change their ways. When they
didn't, He got angry after enduring generations of this and turned to
judgment.

Here's an illustration: A parent asks their child to do something.
The child says okay, but it never gets done. The parent gets tired of

waiting for them to do it. So what happens? The parent passes down judgment, whatever punishment they see fit. If we, as parents, get tired of waiting for minutes, hours, or days, think of how God felt after generations of disobedience. After constantly telling and asking us, being merciful to us, and yet we still continue in our sin. Don't be surprised when He throws His hands in the air and says, "I'm done." How long is He going to put up with a society that rejects Him on a daily basis? He is a loving God, but He is also a righteous God.

Judgment will come. God patiently waits for us to turn to Him. He doesn't force Himself on us. He lets us make our own decisions, even if they are the wrong ones.

"So he got up and came to his father. But while he was still a long way off, his father saw him and felt compassion for him, and ran and embraced him and kissed him" *(Luke 15:20, NASB)*. We all know the return of the prodigal son. This man's son was lost but came back, which brought great joy to his father. As a parent, when your children live far from you, there's joy when they come home. You talk and FaceTime with excitement, but there is joy when they are home, if only for a visit. Now think of the parents whose children are (child is) estranged or lost. The child returns home. How overwhelming it would be, such joy, because they thought they would not see them again. But now they are home. They never stopped waiting for their return.

Our Father is the same way. He waits for us to turn or come back to Him. When we do, He is filled with overwhelming joy. I think there is always a party going on in heaven. They are constantly celebrating the return of a prodigal son.

Patience is enduring and persevering. No matter what we are going through, we have to remember that God keeps His promises. He has never said there won't be suffering or hardships. "For in hope we have been saved, but hope that is seen is not hope; for who hopes for what is already seen? But if we hope for what we do not see, with perseverance, we wait eagerly for it" *(Rom. 8:24–25)*. (Perseverance means steady persistence in the course of action in spite of difficulties, obstacles, or discouragement.)

A married couple is hoping to get pregnant. Once they're pregnant, they are no longer hoping for that. Now they hope for a healthy baby. Once the baby is born, they no longer hope for that. They shift now to the child's future. They can't see the child's future, so they hope for many things for them. During these times of hoping, they were/ are also patiently waiting. They were persevering through the difficulties and/or discouragement. Maybe they weren't getting pregnant, had miscarriages, lots of morning sickness, bed rest, hard labor and delivery, etc.; but they stayed the course and waited for God's perfect timing.

"Therefore, we ourselves speak proudly of you among the churches of God for your perseverance and faith in the midst of all your persecutions and afflictions which you endure" *(2 Thess. 1:4, NASB)*. When we are facing adversity, difficulties, and afflictions, we want God to fix it and handle it right now. But we need to have faith and be persistent while we wait for God and His answers. He may be using this time to draw us closer to Him, maybe use us to be an example for others, or at just the right moment, we are there when someone needs a miracle. People watch us. They see how we react. However, when God uses us, it will be for His glorification, not ours.

"For what credit is there if, when you sin and are harshly treated, you endure it with patience? But if when you do what is right and suffer for it you patiently endure it, this finds favor with God" *(1 Pet. 2:20, NASB)*. God doesn't give us favor when we sin and get treated poorly by others or get punished. We deserve it. We chose to sin. We deserve our judgment. But when we suffer or get treated poorly for doing what is right and setting a good example, that's when we have God's favor. That's when He says, "Well done."

As Christians, we want God's promises and rewards. But we have to wait. It's all in God's timing.

> Then the king said to Haman, "Take quickly the robes and the horse as you have said, and do so for Mordecai the Jew, who is sitting at the king's gate; do not fall short in anything of all that you have said." So Haman took the robe

and the horse, and arrayed Mordecai, and led him on horseback through the city square, and proclaimed before him, "Thus it shall be done to the man whom the king desires to honor." Then Mordecai returned to the king's gate. But Haman hurried home, mourning, with his head covered. Haman recounted to Zeresh his wife and all his friends everything that had happened to him. Then his wise men and Zeresh his wife said to him, "If Mordecai, before whom you have begun to fall, is of Jewish origin, you will not overcome him, but will surely fall before him." (*Esther 6:10–13, NASB*)

Mordecai's reward came at the right time. God used this time so His people would be saved, and the evil man destroyed.

"How will we escape if we neglect so great a salvation? After it was at the first spoken through the Lord, it was confirmed to us by those who heard" *(Heb. 2:3, NASB)*. We can't go on like nothing will ever happen and ignore God's timing by giving up and not being diligent about it. Leave the rest to the Lord to deal with when it comes to others.

Punishment for evil and sin will come. As we look at society today and the evil that is occurring, we have to focus on God's promises. We have to be patient and wait for God's timing. We have to believe and hope in the things not seen and trust in God. There will come a time when Jesus will return. For some, it may be too late. God is patiently waiting for us. He is waiting for us to repent and accept His Son as Lord and Savior. He wants all to be saved.

While writing this, I just had a conversation with my father. He asked me why, with all the evil that is going on (which has gone on for thousands of years), doesn't Jesus just come back and take care of it? My response was because He doesn't want any to perish. He is waiting for as many to repent and accept Him as Lord of all. But how long will He wait? We don't know.

Patience is one of the gifts of the Spirit *(Gal. 5:22)*. As Christians, we should not be trying God's patience, and we should be patient with our fellow man.

Here are some other New Testament scriptures regarding patience:

- "In purity, in knowledge, in patience, in kindness, in the Holy Spirit, in genuine love" *(2 Cor. 6:6, NASB)*.
- "Love is patient, love is kind and is not jealous; love does not brag and is not arrogant" *(1 Cor. 13:4, NASB)*.
- "Preach the word; be ready in season and out of season; reprove, rebuke, exhort, with great patience and instruction" *(2 Tim. 4:2, NASB)*.
- "The Lord's bond-servant must not be quarrelsome, but be kind to all, able to teach, patient when wronged" *(2 Tim. 2:24, NASB)*.

These scriptures all deal with how we relate to each other. We're servants of God, and our character should reflect that. When speaking God's truth, we need to be respectful to avoid foolish debates. When wronged, we must endure without argument, if (at all) possible. God is overwhelmingly patient with us; yet at times, we are not with others. We need to be patient and put our hope and trust in God's timing for all things.

12

Redeemed

There is a song "Let the Redeemed of the Lord Say So." I ask, do the redeemed of the Lord say they are redeemed? Do they know why they are? If they are redeemed, who is their redeemer? How and why did their redemption occur? Let's look at the who, what, why, when, where, and how of being redeemed.

First, what does it mean to be redeemed? To redeem means many things:

- To buy or pay off
- To buy back
- To exchange
- To recover by payment
- To discharge or fulfill (pledge, promise)
- To make up for: make amends for
- To obtain the release or restoration of, from captivity, by paying a ransom
- To deliver from sin and its consequences by means of a sacrifice offered for the sinner

As Christians, we are redeemed by the Lord. We have been recovered by the blood of the Lamb. He made amends for us and fulfilled God's promise. We have been released from our captivity, which is sin. He offered Himself as a sacrifice to deliver us from sin and death. Jesus is our redeemer.

God redeemed His people throughout the Old Testament. In *Exodus 6:6*, God delivered His people from the bondage of the Egyptians. He redeems them with outstretched arms and leads them to the promised land. In *Ruth 4:4*, Boaz redeems Naomi. Boaz, as the next closest kin to Naomi's deceased husband, Elimelek, buys back the land, sold by Naomi to redeem it. Then he marries Ruth, which then raises up the name of the dead, Naomi's husband, thus keeping his inheritance from being lost.

In the same way, God redeems our soul's lost estate, which was lost in the garden of Eden when mankind chose to serve Satan rather than obey God and was doomed to death. All would have been lost because none of us could get it back from Satan's grasp.

"But God will redeem [release, rescue] my soul from the power of death, for He will receive me" *(Ps. 49:15, TLB)*. Christ redeemed us!

"Christ redeemed us from the curse [misfortune, trouble, evil that has been invoked upon one] of the law, having become a curse for us. For it is written, 'Cursed is everyone who hangs on a tree'" *(Gal. 3:13, NASB)*. Through His sacrifice, Christ delivered (set free, liberate, release, save) us from sin and its consequences. He offered up Himself for us the sinners.

"So that He might redeem those under the Law, that we might receive the adoption of sons" *(Gal. 4:5, NASB)*. If one is redeemed, then that would have to mean we have a redeemer (person who redeems). Remember in Ruth 4:4, Naomi's line (through Ruth) was redeemed by Boaz, he was her redeemer.

"Let the words of my mouth and the meditation of my heart, be acceptable in Your sight O Lord, my Rock and my Redeemer" *(Ps. 19:14, NASB)*. David is calling out to God, his redeemer. He wants his words and thoughts to be acceptable to God. This should be our desire. Do we consider whether or not our words are acceptable to God before we speak? If we did, there would be fewer hurt feelings and fewer people who feel offended. More people would feel the love of God.

"Their Redeemer is strong; the LORD of hosts is His name: He shall thoroughly plead their cause, that he may give rest to the land, and disquiet the inhabitants of Babylon" *(Jer. 50:34, KJV)*. The Lord

God is the redeemer throughout the Bible. No one can be redeemed without a ransom. Ransom is a payment in trade for the deliverance, rescue, or salvation of a prisoner.

> Into your hand I commit my spirit; You have ransomed [released, rescued, delivered] me, O LORD God of truth. *(Ps. 31:5, NASB)*

> O draw near to my soul and redeem [buy back, purchase] it; Ransom [deliver, release] me because of my enemies! *(Ps. 69:18, NASB)*

> For the lord has ransomed [purchased, buy back] Jacob and redeemed [rescue, release] him from the hand of him who was stronger than he. *(Jer. 31:11, NASB)*

> For the lord has redeemed [rescued, release] Jacob and ransomed [buy back, purchase] him from the hand that was stronger than he. *(KJV)*

> I will ransom them from the power of the grave; I will redeem them from death; O death; I will be they plagues; O grave, I will be thy destruction: repentance shall be hid from mine eyes. *(Hosea 13:14, KJV)*

Throughout these scriptures, God is the one who has ransomed and redeemed David, Jacob, and Israel. In *Exodus 30:12*, it says, "When thou takest the sum of the children of Israel after their number, then shall they give every man a ransom for his soul unto the Lord, when thou numberest them; that there be no plague among them, when thou numberest them." Ransom is referring to a payment. After the Israelites were numbered, they had to give a ransom (payment) for themselves to the Lord.

"The wicked [guilty, morally wrong, ungodly] shall be a ransom [redemption price, bribe] for the righteous and the transgressor for [in place of] the upright" *(Prov. 21:18, KJV)*. There is a price or exchange being made.

"Who gave Himself as a ransom [redemption price] for (the sake of) all, the testimony given at the proper time" *(1 Tim. 2:6, NASB)*. Who is the "who"? Jesus! Jesus willfully gave Himself (His life) as a ransom (price) for our sins. It was for everyone's sins, His life in exchange for ours. Our salvation was bought. It had a price; it wasn't free. It came at the cost of Jesus's life. It was the ultimate sacrifice, giving up oneself for the sake of someone else. He did it because He loves us.

"Just as the Son of Man did not come to be served, but to serve, and to give His life a ransom [price] for [substitute] many" *(Matt. 20:28, NASB)*. Ransom was a price paid to release a slave from bondage. When Jesus paid our ransom on the cross, He was redeeming (release, rescue) us from the bondage of sin and death. He was our substitute so we would not die but have eternal life with Him. If He didn't, we would all perish. Through Jesus Christ, we have redemption (deliverance from sin and our salvation).

"For the redemption of his soul is costly, and he should cease trying forever" *(Ps. 49:8, NASB)*. We cannot buy eternal life for ourselves or anyone else. Our works will not get us there. Only God can do that, and He did it though the sacrifice of His only Son, Jesus Christ. We cannot bargain, bribe, buy, sell, or trade for salvation or to be set free from sin. Jesus paid that price on the cross.

"But when these things begin to take place, straighten up and lift up your heads because your redemption [rescue] is drawing near" *(Luke 21:28, NASB)*. No matter what is happening in the world, our eyes are to be on Christ and His return. He will bring justice and restoration to his people. We are not to worry. I need to remind myself of this. When I see some things happening, I tend to worry about it instead of focusing on God and His Word and promises. When I stay focused on God, I don't worry because my faith is in Him.

"Being justified as a gift by His grace through the redemption [being set free from sin] which is in Christ Jesus. *(Rom. 3:24, NASB)*.

It's only by God's grace and mercy that we have redemption, and we have been set free from sin. In the Old Testament, not even the next of kin could buy our soul's freedom. *Psalm 49:7* says, "No one can redeem the life of another or give to God a ransom for them," but Christ did that for us.

"And not only this, but also, we ourselves, having the first fruits of the Spirit, even we ourselves groan within ourselves, waiting eagerly for our adoption as sons, the redemption of the body" *(Rom. 8:23, NASB)*. When Jesus left this world, He promised to send a helper. That helper is the Holy Spirit. He is within us as we wait for our resurrected bodies (glorified bodies).

"In Him we have redemption [price paid to have freedom for a slave, deliverance, [rescue] through His blood, the forgiveness of our trespasses according to the riches of His grace" *(Eph. 1:7)*. Before Jesus's sacrifice, we were all slaves to sin and the law. Slaves have no freedom unless they are bought by someone who will set them free. Jesus is that person. He bought our freedom by sacrificing Himself on the cross. It was His blood that was shed freely for us to be delivered, to be forgiven. This was done by God's grace and mercy. It is freely given. There is nothing we can do to earn our salvation. We just have to have faith in Christ.

"He rescued us from the domain of darkness, transferred us to the kingdom of His beloved Son. In whom we have redemption, the forgiveness of sins [because of Jesus's sacrifice]" *(Col. 1:13–14)*. Christ is light, and because He has rescued us and is in us, we are no longer in the darkness. His light is in us. We are His family, and we belong to His kingdom. We went from being slaves to being free, guilty of sin to forgiveness, from the darkness to the light, and from the power of Satan to the power of God. Our life should reflect this. We just have to stay near to God in prayer, in His word, and in His presence.

"And not through the blood of goats and calves [*Old* Testament], but through His own blood He entered the holy place once and for all, having obtained eternal redemption. [*New*

Testament] Through Christ's own death, He freed us from the slavery of sin forever" *(Heb. 9:12).*

By Jesus's blood we have/are

- our conscience cleansed,
- freed from death's sting so we can live to serve God,
- freed from sin's power.

Jesus's sacrifice made animal sacrifice no longer necessary. We need to trust Him and accept His gift of eternal life. Develop a relationship with Him.

Now let's go back to the who, what, where, when, how and why of redemption:

- Who is our redeemer? Jesus Christ, who carried out the plan that the Trinity planned before time on earth began.
- What is the meaning of redeemed? It means being bought back, which includes being released and rescued.
- Where? In the Old Testament, through sacrifices which typified Christ. In the New Testament, on Mount Calvary, where Jesus died. When? From the garden of Eden when the sin of Adam and Eve needed that first sacrifice until Calvary when Jesus died.
- How? By the death of a pure and blameless sacrifice which had no spot nor blemish, a type of Jesus Christ, who was also without sin and totally innocent.
- Why? Because of the love spoken of in *John 3:16,* "For God so loved the world that he gave his one and only Son, that whoever believes in him shall not perish but have eternal life."

13

Obedience

What Does It Mean to Be Obedient?

Here are some definitions:

- The state of being obedient
- The act or practice of obeying, dutiful, or submissive compliance
- A sphere of authority or jurisdiction, especially ecclesiastical
- The act or practice of obeying, dutiful, or submissive compliance
- The act or practice of obeying, dutiful, or submissive compliance
- Chiefly ecclesiastical (relating to church, clergy, clerical; not secular)
  a. Conformity to a monastic rule or the authority of a religious superior, especially on the part of one who has vowed such conformance (comply, act in accord with standards, attitudes, practices of society or group)
  b. The rule or authority that exacts (to call for, demand, require) (precise, strictly accurate) such conformance

The first command given by God to man is found in *Genesis 2:16–17*. God says to not eat from the tree of the knowledge of good and evil. We don't know how long it was between chapter 2 and 3, but chapter 3 records the first disobedience. Adam and Eve have now been disobedient because they ate from the tree. God wanted them to obey, but He gave them free will and choice. Unfortunately, they chose wrong, which resulted in sin and the fall of man. It also kept them from spending their life with God in the garden.

In *Genesis 3:11–13*, God asks them if they had eaten from the tree. Their response is typical: they placed the blame on others. Instead of taking responsibility for their actions, Adam blamed Eve, and Eve blamed the serpent. It's like a kid that gets caught with his hand in the cookie jar and blaming his sibling.

Maybe God's response would have been different if Adam and Eve would have admitted they disobeyed instead of rationalizing their choice. The result of Adam's disobedience was sin. When God speaks, we should obey. But free will gives us the freedom to choose. Just remember there will be consequences. So why should we obey God?

"When Abram was ninety-nine years old, the Lord appeared to him and said, 'I am God Almighty; walk before me faithfully and be blameless'" *(Gen. 17:1)*. We obey because He is God Almighty and because the benefits of our obedience are abundant.

How Do We Learn to Obey?

How did you learn as a child? If we didn't obey our parents, we found out very quickly there would be consequences, and our parents didn't trust us. If we did obey, then our parents trusted us and gradually increased our responsibility. It's the same with God.

> Then the Lord said to Moses, "Behold I will rain bread from heaven for you; and the people shall go out and gather a day's portion every day that I may test them, whether or not they will walk in my instruction. On the 6th day, when they prepare what they bring in, it will be twice as much as they gather daily." *(Exod. 16:4–5)*

God was teaching them to obey. This was a small test of their obedience. Were they going to follow His instruction? Go out and get your portion for the day. No big deal. They would have plenty to eat. But if they gathered more than needed, it showed God they didn't trust Him for their provision each day.

The Lord told me to stop watching a certain show. I tried to bargain with Him, asking why. It's not that bad of a show; it's funny. He didn't budge. Then He said, "How can I trust you to obey in the big things I ask of you if you aren't going to obey in the little." If we aren't obedient in the little things, then He will probably never use us for the big things. How many of us would trust someone with something important if we couldn't trust them with something menial? We wouldn't, and neither will God. He starts us with small things to teach us to obey and then gradually adds more. He wants to know that He can trust us as much as we want to know that we can trust Him.

All of us have been obedient throughout our life. But none of us have been obedient to death except Jesus, our Lord and Savior.

> "Being found in appearance as a man, He humbled Himself by becoming obedient to the point of death, even death on a cross" *(Phil. 2:8)*. Why?

"For as through one man's disobedience the many were made sinner, even so through the obedience of the One the many were made righteous" *(Rom. 5:19)*. Jesus knew the great pain and suffering He would endure and submitted to His Father's will anyway. Jesus was obedient (submissive compliance, practice of obeying) to His Father's authority because He knew this was the way for us to be righteous, to have eternal life with Him. Jesus was off about obeying His Father's will, unlike the righteous leaders of His time. They conformed (comply, act in accord with standards, attitudes, practices of society and groups) to the high priest and their own set of standards, rules, attitudes, and practices. They also called (required, demanded) their followers to do the same. They weren't interested in their Father's will. They were concerned about themselves, their synagogues, and temple money.

In today's society, are our churches and church leaders like Jesus by submitting and obeying our Father's will? Or are they like the Pharisees and only concerned with themselves and keeping their flock, in essence, submitting to their own authority. I believe there are both types, and each will have consequences, good or bad.

When We Are Obedient

Is it because it is our duty, out of fear, or out of love. Is it in our heart?

> Then he took the book of the covenant and read it in the hearing of the people; and they said, "All that the Lord has spoken we will do, and we will be obedient!" *(Exod. 24:7)*

> And He said, "Who told you that you were naked? Have you eaten from the tree of which I commanded you not to eat?" The man said, "The woman whom You gave to be with me, she gave me from the tree, and I ate." Then the Lord God said to the woman, "What is this you have done?" And the woman said, "The serpent deceived me, and I ate." *(Gen. 3:11–13)*

We are to obey God not only because He tells us to, but also, shouldn't we do it because we love and trust Him?

"So Abraham rose early in the morning and saddled his donkey, and took two of his young men with him and Isaac his son; and he split wood for the burnt offering, and arose and went to the place of which God had told him" *(Gen. 22:3)*. God asks Abraham to offer up his son as a sacrifice. Can you imagine how that would tear you up as a parent? But Abraham knew to trust God in all things. He obeyed.

God now knew Abraham loved Him even more than his own son. God rewarded him by providing another sacrifice and blessing him abundantly.

There will be times that God will ask us to give up something important to us. Will we obey? Or will it be more important than God?

> Then the king commanded Hilkiah the high priest and the priests of the second order and the doorkeepers, to bring out of the temple of the Lord all the vessels that were made for Baal, for Asherah, and for all the host of heaven; and he burned them outside Jerusalem in the fields of the Kidron, and carried their ashes to Bethel. He did away with the idolatrous priests whom the kings of Judah had appointed to burn incense in the high places in the cities of Judah and in the surrounding area of Jerusalem, also those who burned incense to Baal, to the sun and to the moon and to the constellations and to all the host of heaven. He brought out the Asherah from the house of the Lord outside Jerusalem to the brook Kidron, and burned it at the brook Kidron, and ground it to dust, and threw its dust on the graves of the common people. He also broke down the houses of the male cult prostitutes which were in the house of the Lord, where the women were weaving hangings for the Asherah. Then he brought all the priests from the cities of Judah, and defiled the high places where the priests had burned incense, from Geba to Beersheba; and he broke down the high places of the gates which were at the entrance of the gate of Joshua the governor of the city, which were on one's left at the city gate. *(2 Kings 23:4–8)*

Josiah didn't just say he would obey, he actually did it. Josiah did what faith requires action and obedience.

"Before him there was no king like him who turned to the Lord with all his heart and with all his soul and with all his might, according to all the law of Moses; nor did any like him arise after him" *(2 Kings 23:25)*. Josiah loved the Lord with all his heart, soul, and might and obeyed the laws according to Moses. He kept God's covenant. He was obedient. He recognized sin, eliminated sinful practices, and attacked the cause of sin. We need to be like Josiah. Obedient to God's Word and recognize the sin in our lives. Then we need to get rid of and eliminate that sin. We have to look at what is causing us to sin (relationship, pattern, routine). When we know the cause, then we must attack it with God's Holy Spirit power within us. Will we be a slave to sin or to Jesus?

> Do you not know that when you present yourselves to someone as slaves for obedience, you are slaves of the one whom you obey, either of sin resulting in death, or of obedience resulting in righteousness? But thanks be to God that though you were slaves of sin, you became obedient from the heart to that form of teaching to which you were committed. *(Rom. 6:16–17)*

We are no longer slaves to sin because of our salvation in Jesus Christ. God wants our hearts and must come into all areas of our life. It can't be partial.

> So Jesus said to them, "Children, you do not have any fish, do you?" They answered Him, "No." And He said to them, "Cast the net on the right-hand side of the boat and you will find a catch." So they cast, and then they were not able to haul it in because of the great number of fish. *(John 21:5–6)*

He who has My commandments and keeps them is the one who loves Me; and he who loves Me will be loved by My Father, and I will love him and will disclose Myself to him. *(John 14:21)*

Therefore I urge you, brethren, by the mercies of God, to present your bodies a living and holy sacrifice, acceptable to God, which is your spiritual service of worship. *(Rom. 12:1)*

Samuel said, "Has the Lord as much delight in burnt offerings and sacrifices as in obeying the voice of the Lord? Behold, to obey is better than sacrifice, And to heed than the fat of rams. For rebellion is as the sin of divination, and insubordination is as iniquity and idolatry. Because you have rejected the word of the Lord, He has also rejected you from being king." *(1 Sam. 15:22–23)*

God would rather us obey Him than offer up a hallow sacrifice. He wants our hearts. Being religious isn't enough if we aren't devoted to God. He wants us to obey Him because we love Him. We want to please those we love. It doesn't matter what a person looks like on the outside. God knows our hearts and if we are sincere or not. When we accepted Him into our lives, we committed ourselves to Him and prove it by obeying His Word.

"Then he took the book of the covenant and read it in the hearing of the people; and they said, 'All that the Lord has spoken we will do, and we will be obedient'" *(Exod. 24:7)*! It is also pleasing to the Lord when we obey.

Children, be obedient to your parents in all things, for this is well-pleasing to the Lord. *(Col. 3:20)*

"Woe to you, scribes and Pharisees, hypo-
crites! For you tithe mint and dill and cummin,
and have neglected the weightier provisions of
the law: justice and mercy and faithfulness; but
these are the things you should have done without neglecting the others. You blind guides, who
strain out a gnat and swallow a camel!" *(Matt.
23:23–24)*

The scribes and Pharisee would obey details of their laws but
neglect and be disobedient to the more important things like justice,
mercy, and faithfulness. They were so concerned with keeping their
outside clean that they neglected their inside (the heart).

We need to make sure we are obedient in all areas of our lives.
We can't pick and choose when we want to obey. We can't have
that outward obedience without a change of heart. The scribes and
Pharisees acted like they were obedient to the law, but their hearts
were far from it. They put themselves above everyone. They were
self-righteous, pious, and self-centered. It was all about them and not
God. That would be like the person who goes to church so people
think he's a Christian. It's not about appearances; it's about what's in
our hearts. It's because we love the Lord.

Luke 17:7–10 says it's our duty to be obedient. Slaves are to do
what they are commanded. So if we are slaves to Christ, we should be
doing what He commands, and we should be doing it out of love for
Him. We should see it as a privilege to serve Him and others.

"Since you have in obedience to the truth purified your souls
for a sincere love of the brethren, fervently love one another from the
heart" *(1 Pet. 1:22)*. Since you have in obedience to the truth (Jesus)
purified your souls for a sincere love of the brethren, fervently love
one another from the heart. Jesus commanded us to love one another
as He has loved us. If His love is in our hearts then loving one another
should be easy. But God gave us free will and unfortunately with free
will can come disobedience.

"Then Pharaoh summoned Moses and Aaron and said, 'Go,
sacrifice to your God here in the land'" *(Exod. 8:25)*. Pharaoh told

Moses he could go sacrifice within the land. But God told Moses to go into the wilderness. Pharaoh offered a compromise. Moses would not.

When it comes to obeying God's command, there is no compromise. If God tells us to give something up or to go somewhere, we can't say, "Oh, I will give up part of it," or "I'll just go here. It's almost there." For example: "You asked me to stop smoking, so I will only smoke one cigarette a day."

Compromising Is Not Being Obedient

We can't choose to obey one part but not the other. We have to be committed and obedient to the whole thing. How frustrating is it when you ask someone to do something and they take their old sweet time getting around to doing it with no regard for your wishes. I am sure we all get a little steamed. How patient are we while we wait? But when God tells us to go or do this, we make Him wait. Slow response isn't much better than disobedience, and there are consequences.

When he hesitated, the men grasped his hand and the hands of his wife and of his two daughters and led them safely out of the city, for the Lord was merciful to them" *(Gen. 19:16, NIV)*. Lot was told to leave because God was going to destroy Sodom and Gomorrah. But he hesitated. They had to seize them by the hand to get them outside the city.

The Lord had compassion on him, so why did he hesitate? Did he not want to give up his stuff, prestige, comfort? When God tells us to do something, do we hesitate? Do we look at the things we will leave behind (worldly enticements)? Are they more important than what God wants? Lot's wife must have thought so. She looked back (disobeyed) and lost her life. Slow obedience isn't good enough.

> In the morning, however, they rose up early and went up to the ridge of the hill country, saying, "Here we are; we have indeed sinned, but we will go up to the place which the Lord has

promised." But Moses said, "Why then are you transgressing the commandment of the Lord, when it will not succeed? Do not go up, or you will be struck down before your enemies, for the Lord is not among you. For the Amalekites and the Canaanites will be there in front of you, and you will fall by the sword, inasmuch as you have turned back from following the Lord. And the Lord will not be with you." But they went up heedlessly to the ridge of the hill country; neither the ark of the covenant of the Lord nor Moses left the camp. *(Num. 14:40–44)*

The sons of Israel decided too late to go to the place that the Lord had promised. Since they didn't go when the Lord commanded, He would no longer be among them if they went.

God isn't going to wait for us. If we don't obey His command, He will find someone who will, and we may miss out on whatever He had planned for us. We not only have to do what is right, but we also have to do it at the right time, or God won't be with us either.

"He gathered the priests and Levites and said to them, 'Go out to the cities of Judah and collect money from all Israel to repair the house of your God annually, and you shall do the matter quickly.' But the Levites did not act quickly" *(2 Chron. 24:5)*. Joash told the priests and Levites to collect money from Israel so they could repair the house of God. They were to do it quickly. They did not. They disregarded Joash and God.

How long will God continue to be disregarded before He distances Himself from us?

"But Jonah rose up to flee to Tarshish from the presence of the Lord. So he went down to Joppa, found a ship which was going to Tarshish, paid the fare and went down into it to go with them to Tarshish from the presence of the Lord" *(Jonah 1:3)*. Jonah didn't obey God right away; he fled from Him. Jonah didn't want to do what God was asking Him to do. Why? Because God told him to go and preach to Nineveh, but Nineveh was a cruel, oppressive enemy of Jonah's nation. Jonah knew that if they repented, God would save them. He didn't want them saved. "Therefore in order to forestall this I fled to Tarshish, for I knew that You are a gracious and compassionate God, slow to anger and abundant in lovingkindness, and one who relents concerning calamity" *(Jon. 4:2)*. Why don't we do what God asks? Jonah's disobedience just led him into more trouble. He endangered the lives of others and spent three days in the belly of a whale. It was only then that Jonah realized he could have saved himself a lot of trouble if he would have just obeyed to begin with.

We can run from God, but we can't hide. The more we run, the more trouble we bring upon ourselves and others. This is not what God wants. It's what we bring through disobedience. Our lives will be more peaceful if we obey from the beginning.

We really have to hang on to our faith and the power of the Holy Spirit when obeying God. There will be times of opposition, difficulty, problems; and it may seem impossible, but God is with us.

> But the king of Egypt said to them, "Moses and Aaron, why do you draw the people away from their work? Get back to your labors!" Again Pharaoh said, "Look, the people of the land are now many, and you would have them cease from their labors!" So the same day Pharaoh commanded the taskmasters over the people and their foremen, saying, "You are no longer to give the people straw to make brick as previously; let them go and gather straw for themselves. But the quota of bricks which they were making previously, you shall impose on them; you are not to reduce any of it. Because they are lazy, therefore they cry out, 'Let us go and sacrifice to our God.' Let the labor be heavier on the men, and let them work at it so that they will pay no attention to false words. *(Exod. 5:4–9)*

In this passage, Moses and Aaron were doing what God told them to do. However, Pharaoh made it harder on the people. God never said that obedience would guarantee a life of ease, lacking any struggle. Sometimes opposition comes because you are doing what is right.

How faithful are we when God calls? Do we see it as impossible?

> Now the Lord spoke to Moses, saying, "Go, tell Pharaoh, king of Egypt to let the sons of Israel go out of his land." But Moses spoke before the Lord, saying, "Behold, the sons of Israel have not listened to me; how then will Pharaoh listen to me, for I am unskilled in speech?" *(Exod. 6:10–12)*

Moses is whining to the Lord, "Israel isn't listening to me, so why would Pharaoh?" He says that he's not good with words. He's trying to get out of it by making excuses.

We have to remember that God will equip us to do whatever He asks. When setbacks occur, we have to focus on God.

When We Obey, Expect Opposition

Evil doesn't want us to obey. The book of Joshua records a time that Joshua disobeyed, having not prayed about the guests who visited his camp. He mistakenly made a covenant with those God told him to destroy.

> Now it came about when all the kings who were beyond the Jordan, in the hill country and in the lowland and on all the coast of the Great Sea toward Lebanon, the Hittite and the Amorite, the Canaanite, the Perizzite, the Hivite and the Jebusite, heard of it, that they gathered themselves together with one accord to fight

with Joshua and with Israel. When the inhabitants of Gibeon heard what Joshua had done to Jericho and to Ai, they also acted craftily and set out as envoys, and took worn-out sacks on their donkeys, and wineskins worn-out and torn and mended, and worn-out and patched sandals on their feet, and worn-out clothes on themselves; and all the bread of their provision was dry and had become crumbled. They went to Joshua to the camp at Gilgal and said to him and to the men of Israel, "We have come from a far country; now therefore, make a covenant with us." *(Josh. 9:1–6)*

In the New Testament, the disciples were forbidden by the Sanhedrin to preach in Jesus's name, but notice their answer: "But Peter and the apostles answered, 'We must obey God rather than men'" *(Acts 5:29)*. Again, when we obey, expect opposition. The evil one doesn't want us to obey. He will do anything to stop us. We have to stay strong in the Lord.

In *Luke 1:38, an angel visits Mary and informs her that she is going to bear a child, born not of man, but of God.* "And Mary said, 'Behold, the bondslave of the Lord; may it be done to me according to your word.' And the angel departed from her." Mary didn't hesitate. She knew what it would mean for her to be pregnant and betrothed. She accepted on her faith and trusted in the Lord. This was not going to be easy. There was opposition, difficulty, struggles; and it seemed impossible. Even so, she put her trust in the Lord. She didn't focus on those other things. She was humbled to be asked by God to carry His Son. And she obeyed. We have to be consistent in our obedience.

King Saul began well but strayed from obedience. *First Samuel 31* tells of the death of Saul, who had built a history of disobedience. He and his sons paid for it in his death. In contrast, David ended his life having been faithful. In his old age, one of his last acts is seen in *2 Chronicles 26:20–22*:

> Then David said to all the assembly, "Now bless the Lord your God." And all the assembly blessed the Lord, the God of their fathers, and bowed low and did homage to the Lord and to the king. On the next day they made sacrifices to the Lord and offered burnt offerings to the Lord, 1,000 bulls, 1,000 rams and 1,000 lambs, with their drink offerings and sacrifices in abundance for all Israel. So they ate and drank that day before the Lord with great gladness.

Both Saul, and later Uzziah, had times of obedience; but they also turned away from God, and judgment came.

We can't be wishy-washy. It is lifelong obedience that is required, not just when we feel like it. That is disobedience.

Obedience to God Opens Us Up

Obedience to God opens us up to His care, miracles, success, peace, and freedom. But we also must humble ourselves and take the first step.

In *Joshua 3:13–14*, God said,

> "It shall come about when the soles of the feet of the priests who carry the ark of the Lord, the Lord of all the earth, rest in the waters of the Jordan, the waters of the Jordan will be cut off, and the waters which are flowing down from above will stand in one heap." So when the people set out from their tents to cross the Jordan with the priests carrying the ark of the covenant before the people.

When crossing into the promised land, God gave Joshua instructions. Once the priests stepped into the river, it would stop so the people could cross. They trusted God, were obedient, and crossed on dry land. If they wouldn't have taken that first step into the river and trusted God, would they have gone into the promised land? Would God have sent them back into the wilderness because of their disobedience? We don't know. The Jordan River was their obstacle. What are ours? Do we see them as impossible to cross? We have to remember nothing is impossible for God. Our trust must be in Him. We need to take that first step in faith, and God will provide a solution to our situation/problem.

God wants to care for us. *Deuteronomy 11* tells how God wants to bless His people. In *Exodus 15:26*, there is another example: "And He said, 'If you will give earnest heed to the voice of the Lord your God, and do what is right in His sight, and give ear to His commandments, and keep all His statutes, I will put none of the diseases on you which I have put on the Egyptians; for I, the Lord, am your healer.'" "Earnest heed" means (1) serious, intense, not joking, zealous, sincere, deeply convinced, (2) important, (3) pledge in binding a bargain.

Give earnest heed to God's voice. Are we serious, zealous, and sincere to hear God? Is it important to keep His statutes? If we do, is it our pledge to Him and our part of the bargain so He will continue to care for us and be our healer? We cannot compromise.

God wants us to succeed, but we have to be obedient to His commands to do so.

> Be strong and courageous, for you shall give this people possession of the land which I swore to their fathers to give them. Only be strong and very courageous; be careful to do according to all the law which Moses My servant commanded you; do not turn from it to the right or to the left, so that you may have success wherever you go. This book of the law shall not depart from your mouth, but you shall meditate on it day and

night, so that you may be careful to do according
to all that is written in it; for then you will make
your way prosperous, and then you will have success. *(Josh. 1:6–80)*

God is commanding Joshua to be strong and courageous and
do all that the Law of Moses commanded him to do. If Joshua didn't
veer to the right or the left, he would be successful wherever he went.
God is saying the same to us. If we will obey His commands and stay
on His righteous path, we will always be successful. The problem in
today's society is that there is a warped sense of what it means to be
successful. The world looks at jobs, money, power, number of cars,
what you dress like, etc. These mean nothing.

Sure, we need some of these, but it doesn't represent our success in life. Success: (a) favorable/prosperous termination of attempts
or endeavors, the accomplishment of one's goals; (b) attainment of
wealth, position, honors.

Is success wealth? Is it a great quantity of money, valuable possessions, property, or other riches? Is it the abundance or profusion
(great quantity) of anything in a plentiful amount? As Christians,
we can't measure success the same way the world does. Our success
might not be measured here but in heaven. We may not see things
as being a success but God might. Wealth is anything in a plentiful
amount. As Christians, we have God's grace, mercy, forgiveness, and
love in a plentiful amount. I would say we are successful.

Obedience Leads to Peace

So Abijah slept with his fathers, and they
buried him in the city of David, and his son Asa
became king in his place. The land was undisturbed for ten years during his days. Asa did good
and right in the sight of the Lord his God, for he
removed the foreign altars and high places, tore
down the sacred pillars, cut down the Asherim,

and commanded Judah to seek the Lord God of their fathers and to observe the law and the commandment. He also removed the high places and the incense altars from all the cities of Judah. And the kingdom was undisturbed under him. He built fortified cities in Judah, since the land was undisturbed, and there was no one at war with him during those years, because the Lord had given him rest. *(2 Chron. 14:1–6)*

Asa did right in the sight of the Lord. He tore down foreign altars, high places, sacred pillars, and asherim. He commanded Judah to seek the Lord God and observe His laws and commandments. Because of his devotion and obedience to God, the Lord gave him rest. How sweet to rest in the Lord. When we seek the Lord and are obedient, God will give us peace, even in times of distress and trouble. There have been times in my life when God's peace is all that kept me sane.

Obedience Can Lead to Miracles and Freedom

So he arose and went to Zarephath, and when he came to the gate of the city, behold, a widow was there gathering sticks; and he called to her and said, "Please get me a little water in a jar, that I may drink." As she was going to get it, he called to her and said, "Please bring me a piece of bread in your hand." But she said, "As the Lord your God lives, I have no bread, only a handful of flour in the bowl and a little oil in the jar; and behold, I am gathering a few sticks that I may go in and prepare for me and my son, that we may eat it and die." Then Elijah said to her, "Do not fear; go, do as you have said, but make me a little bread cake from it first and bring it out to me, and afterward you may make one for yourself and for your son. For thus says the Lord God of Israel, The bowl of flour shall not be exhausted, nor shall the jar of oil be empty, until the day that the Lord sends rain on the face of the earth." So she went and did according to the word of Elijah, and she and he and her household ate for many days. The bowl of flour was not exhausted nor did the jar of oil become empty, according to the word of the Lord which He spoke through Elijah. *(1 Kings 17:10–16)*

Elijah told the widow to make a cake for him and bring it, then make one for her and her son. Even though she didn't have enough, she obeyed Elijah and trusted in the Lord. The Lord then performed a miracle because her bowl of flour and jar of oil never ran out. However, for the miracle to happen, she had to be obedient. Now I know we all don't get the miracles we want. God has His reasons. But if we are disobedient, will that stop a miracle from happening? This widow and her son would have died if she disobeyed Elijah.

We Need to Obey

We need to obey even when we don't understand why. David was carrying the ark back to Israel and didn't carry it properly. Uzza was killed instantly when he touched it *(1 Chron. 15:13–15)*. David then went back and corrected his mistake to follow the proper procedures for carrying the ark.

There are times when certain procedures/rules are to be followed and we don't know why. In faith, we are to just follow God's instruction. He had His reasons. "For my thoughts are not your thoughts, neither are your ways my ways, saith the Lord. For as the heavens are higher than the earth, so are my ways higher than your ways, and my thoughts than your thoughts" *(Isa. 55:8–9, KJV)*.

What happens when you try to put something together without reading the instructions? If it's like my house, it will probably fall apart. But if you follow the instructions, it fits together, and you have a finished product. Do we question the instructions or just follow them? So why do we question God's instructions? His blueprint is in His Word. Yet we don't always want to follow it. He tells us to do something, and we question why. What kind of finished product are we going to be if we aren't put together by His instruction?

Obeying Isn't Always Easy

It takes faith, strength, and courage. Sometimes God will ask us to do extraordinary things. And it will be hard to do.

"When the Lord began to speak through Hosea, the Lord said to him, 'Go, marry a promiscuous woman and have children with her, for like an adulterous wife this land is guilty of unfaithfulness to the Lord.' So he married Gomer daughter of Diblaim, and she conceived and bore him a son" *(Hosea 1:2–3, NIV)*. Hosea was told to go take a wife of harlotry (a prostitute) and have children. I can only imagine what Hosea must have thought at first. "Really, God, you want me, your prophet, to marry a harlot. Not only that, but have children with her?" He might not have wanted to, but he did obey.

We can't forget that God has a plan that we don't always see and understand. We just have to trust and obey. Sometimes the benefit will be for others and not for us. What He asks might be difficult. When that happens, will we obey like Hosea and trust God?

Obedience Must Come into All Areas

Obedience must come into all areas of our life, not just some of them.

> Woe to you, teachers of the law and
> Pharisees, you hypocrites! You give a tenth of

your spices—mint, dill and cumin. But you have neglected the more important matters of the law—justice, mercy and faithfulness. You should have practiced the latter, without neglecting the former. You blind guides! You strain out a gnat but swallow a camel. *(Matt. 23:23–24, NIV)*

The scribes and Pharisees would obey details of their laws but neglect and be disobedient to the more important things, like justice, mercy, and faithfulness. They were so concerned with keeping their outside clean that they neglected their inside vessel (the heart). We need to make sure we are obedient in all areas of our lives. We can't pick and choose when we want to obey (for example, I will go to church, but I won't tithe).

We Can't Have That Outward Obedience

We can't have that outward obedience without a change of heart. The scribes and Pharisees acted like they were obedient to the law, but their hearts were far from it. They put themselves above everyone. They were pompous, and their hearts weren't changed. They didn't have love in their heart. They were self-righteous, pious, and self-centered. It was all about them and not God. That would be like the person who goes to church so people think he's a Christian. But it's not about how we appear to others; it's about what's in your heart. It's because we love the Lord.

We Need to Be Obedient from the Heart

"The law was brought in so that the trespass might increase. But where sin increased, grace increased all the more" *(Rom. 5:20, NIV)*. As the law came, we learned more and more what we were doing was wrong and recognized even more how desperately we needed God's grace. We have the freedom to obey out of love through God's power.

"Therefore, although in Christ I could be bold and order you to do what you ought to do, yet I prefer to appeal to you on the basis of love. It is as none other than Paul—an old man and now also a prisoner of Christ Jesus" *(Philem. 1:8–9, NIV)*. Paul was telling Philemon, "I am an apostle, I could order you to do what is right [in dealing with Onesimus], but I would rather you do what's right because you love Jesus. You know that's what He would do." He wouldn't want him to act grudgingly; He would want heartfelt obedience.

How often do we do things grudgingly? We know it's the right thing to do, but we don't want to do it. Our heart's not in it. God wants our heart. He always has a purpose when asking us to do something. Maybe we are to be that final divine appointment for someone, but because it's an inconvenience to our day, we have a very negative attitude (our heart isn't in it), and the appointment is lost. We need to be doing God's will with our whole heart. It is the right thing to do.

"He did what was right in the eyes of the Lord, but not wholeheartedly" *(2 Chron. 25:2, NIV)*. How often do you get frustrated when you ask someone to do something and they do it halfheartedly? It's done, but not very well. When we go to work, do we just go and do our job? Or do we do it to the best of our ability?

God wants us to do what's right because we love Him. But how many just go through the motions, do our duty and that's it? Why go to church if you don't really want to be there? You can fool people, but you can't fool God. He knows our hearts. If we grudgingly do something, it's not true obedience.

Unfortunately, there are many that are more concerned with seeking others approval verses obeying God. "And Joseph awoke from his sleep and did as the Angel of the Lord commanded him and took Mary as his wife" *(Matt. 1:24)*. By law, Joseph didn't have to marry Mary. He could have had her stoned. He knew the truth of Mary's conception. Others disapproved, but Joseph chose to do the right thing no matter what others thought.

Are we concerned with what others might think or say over what God says? We need to do what God says is right over the approval of others.

It took me some time to really comprehend this. As I look back, there were things I would choose based on if I thought my father would approve. I grew up with four brothers and one sister, and it seemed to always be about the boys. It might not have been, but that was my perception. As my relationship with the Lord grew, I began to realize my choices and decisions needed to please Him *and* my father. Even more than my dad's approval, I first and foremost needed God's approval. I was now looking to my heavenly Father for approval and making my choices based on His truth. That was what mattered.

"Paul, a servant of Jesus Christ, called to be an apostle, separated unto the gospel of God" *(Rom. 1:1)*. The word used here for *servant* was the word for a *bondservant*. A bondservant could go free, but because he cared about his master, he chose to stay. We are to be a bondservant (a person who voluntarily serves) of Jesus. We are to be completely dependent on Him. Only by doing so can He use us to do His work.

Luke 17:7–10 says it's our duty to be obedient. Slaves are to do what they are commanded. So if we are slaves to Christ, we should be doing what He commands. But we should also be doing it out of our love for Him. We should see it as a privilege to serve Him and others.

Obedience May Lead to Suffering

> Son though he was, he learned obedience
> from what he suffered. *(Heb. 5:8, NIV)*

For just as through the disobedience of the one man the many were made sinners, so also through the obedience of the one man the many will be made righteous. *(Rom. 5:19)*

Jesus chose to obey even though it led to great suffering and death. He continually made the will of His Father His own. His suffering and death make it possible for us to endure suffering through our faith and trust in Him. He understands our struggles and wants us to lean on His Holy Spirit strength.

As we grow in the Lord, we may seem different to those in the world. "By faith Noah, when warned about things not yet seen, in holy fear built an ark to save his family. By his faith he condemned the world and became heir of the righteousness that is in keeping with faith" *(Heb. 11:7, NIV)*.

Noah obeyed God and built the ark. I am sure people were mocking, laughing, and cursing him. However, he stayed faithful to God. His walk was different from the rest of the world. When our walk is different from those around us, people will start to reject us. Our obedience makes their disobedience standout.

We Need to Obey to Continue

We need to obey to continue to follow God. So where do we find the strength to obey? "He took Peter and the two sons of Zebedee along with him, and he began to be sorrowful and troubled. Then he said to them, 'My soul is overwhelmed with sorrow to the point of death. Stay here and keep watch with me'" *(Matt. 26:37–38)*. Jesus is in the garden knowing very well what will soon be coming, the pain, the suffering, the separation from His Father, and even His death. He didn't run. He prayed to His Father and received His strength—the same place we can get ours, Abba Father.

John the Baptist was obedient to God's call on his life. He had a specific role/job, and he put all of himself into that task. He announced the coming of the Savior and spoke God's truth. John was in the desert when God's call came to him. He was ready and waiting.

Are we preparing ourselves for God's call? Will we be prepared and ready to go? Will you be obedient? If not, He will call someone who is.

"He that saith he abideth in him ought himself also so to walk, even as he walked" *(1 John 2:6, KJV)*. Abide in Jesus. Obey His teachings. If we abide in Jesus, then we should walk like Him. Obey His teachings, and follow His example of complete obedience to God and loving service to people.

"And now also the axe is laid unto the root of the trees: therefore every tree which bringeth not forth good fruit is hewn down, and cast into the fire" *(Matt. 3:10, KJV)*. We need to be productive in our Christian life and obedient because if we are not bearing fruit, we will be cut off like a tree that doesn't bear fruit.

How to obey:

- With our heart: love Him more than anything.
- With our will: commit ourselves completely to Him.
- With our mind: seek to know Him and His Word so it is the foundation of all we think and do.
- With our body: recognize our strengths, talents, and sexuality are given to us by God to be used according to His rules, not ours.
- With our finances: all our resources ultimately come from God.
- With our future: life's work and main purpose to make service to God and people.

ABOUT THE AUTHOR

This is the first collaboration for Tom and Maureen. They have been married for thirty-seven years and are blessed with three children and three grandchildren. Tom has a son by a previous marriage, and he has four children. Tom has been a longtime high school coach and has received many honors. In addition to coaching championship teams and individuals, he is a member of two Hall of Fames. Maureen is also a great athlete with nine varsity letters in three years. She presently teaches high school health and physical education. In this first effort, both feel their words come from God. The book has been a long time coming, but God's timing is always perfect.